MEDICAL AND DENTAL .

With compliments from the medical newspaper, Doctor

Doctor is the only medical newspaper with a Scottish edition, which was launched in recognition of the fact that GPs in Scotland face a separate set of challenges following devolution of power to the Scottish Parliament. A special edition has allowed **Doctor** to meet the specific information needs of Scottish doctors following the Scottish White Paper, Designed to Care, and the development of local health care co-operatives. Other health issues are also covered in depth, such as the problems of recruitment and out-of-hours care facing Scottish GPs in rural areas. **Doctor** has also become a key arena for opinion-forming during a period of rapid change, with a regular section and special supplements on the primary care reforms, in-depth features and a weekly column by the influential Scottish GP Dr Brian Keighley.

**Look in Doctor every Thursday—
the magazine that works harder for GPs**

MEDICAL AND DENTAL NEGLIGENCE

Robert H. Dickson

Sheriff of South Strathclyde, Dumfries and Galloway at Airdrie

Foreword by John R. Griffiths, WS
Solicitor

T&T CLARK
EDINBURGH
1997

T&T CLARK LTD
59 GEORGE STREET
EDINBURGH EH2 2LQ
SCOTLAND

First published 1997
Reprinted 1999

ISBN 0 567 00521 6

British Library Cataloguing-in-Publication Data
A catalogue record for this book is available from the British Library

This special edition is published by T&T Clark
on behalf of the Scottish edition of **Doctor** Magazine

Typeset by Waverley Typesetters, Galashiels
Printed and bound in Great Britain by MPG Books Ltd, Bodmin

Contents

Foreword

Whatever the reasons, it is clear that complaints, claims and litigations against doctors and dentists continue to increase. The particular value of this book is that, in a practical and no-nonsense format, it presents to the reader information about the law and guidance as to practice in advising not only on the law relating to medical and dental negligence but also on the new NHS complaints procedures, fatal accident inquiries and the roles and operation of the General Medical Council and the General Dental Council. Solicitors advising clients who feel they have a grievance against a doctor or dentist should be fully aware of these matters.

Sheriff Dickson is well qualified to write this book. For many years he was solicitor to the Medical and Dental Defence Union of Scotland and so acquired enviable experience in this field of law and practice. Latterly, as a sheriff, he has continued to pursue this interest and has presided over a significant number of medical fatal accident inquiries.

Perhaps the most valuable single emphasis in the book is on the potential difficulties which face a claimant or pursuer in seeking to bring a successful action for damages against a doctor or dentist. Lawyers acting for such clients owe it to them (and to themselves) to explain these difficulties clearly at the outset.

This is a thoroughly useful book and I have no hesitation in recommending it.

J. R. Griffiths
Chairman
Accreditation Panel for Specialism in Medical Negligence
The Law Society of Scotland
7th February 1997

Preface

No field of legal practice has expanded so rapidly in the last few years as that of medical and dental negligence. The latest figures released by the defence societies and health boards show that in 10 years some categories of claims have more than tripled in volume and delictual awards can now exceed £1 million per claim.

As I have always retained an interest in this branch of the law I was persuaded to gather together some of the cases and principles on which Scottish courts rely. I hope that this will be of some assistance to the growing number of practitioners—legal, medical and dental—who now have to be aware of how such litigation is approached by judges and sheriffs.

I experienced just how fast the pace of change was when I found that in the course of the nine months that this text had been in production, two Acts of Parliament, three sets of statutory regulations, the decisions in *Law Hospital NHS Trust* v *Lord Advocate* and in *McFarlane* v *Tayside Health Board*, as well as a *volte face* by the Scottish Legal Aid Board on the subject of certificates for fatal accident inquiries, have precipitated a number of major redrafts. I have endeavoured to reflect the position as at 31st October 1996.

The book is unashamedly Scottish. There have been a number of excellent guides to the position in England, but perhaps owing to the clarity of *Hunter* v *Hanley* and the fact that the number of Scottish claims has only recently mushroomed, there has been no textbook until now devoted solely to this particular element of Scots law.

Robert H. Dickson
31st January 1997

Acknowledgements

Medical Negligence: An Introduction, the booklet recording the text of the Law Society of Scotland PQLE lecture given in 1981 by J. A. Cameron, QC (now Lord Abernethy), gave practitioners in Scotland a compact guide to the subject. I am grateful to him for allowing me to use it as a foundation on which to show the changes since then and to expand the scope of the subject to include the growing field of dental negligence.

The help which I have had from the council and the secretariat of the Medical and Dental Defence Union of Scotland (MDDUS) in allowing me access to records and in supplying me with details is gratefully acknowledged.

Miss Alexandra Campbell, FRCSE, very kindly read the text and her comments and advice have I am sure prevented certain glaring errors. Without the help of a large number of people, including Miss Veronica McManus, Mrs Judith Gallacher, Mrs Mary O'Neill, Miss Helen Philcox, Professor Sheila McLean, Professor Sir David Mason, Mr Ranald Macdonald and Mr James Watt, any flaws would have been far greater.

All this help would have been to little avail without a sympathetic publisher and an understanding editor. I owe a debt of gratitude to them in guiding a fledgling author.

My greatest thanks, however, go to my wife and my son. Sheena offered me constant support and patience and Graeme's technical knowledge got me through the angst of switching the computer on. Without him the book would have no footnotes or even paragraphs!

The book is dedicated to the memory of Dr James (Pat) Patterson, who until his untimely death in 1986 was the Secretary of the MDDUS. He was responsible for sparking the interest within me for this field of law. His advice and sympathy was appreciated by thousands of doctors and dentists, as they were by me throughout our working relationship and long friendship.

RHD

Table of Cases

Table of Statutes

Table of Statutory Instruments and Circulars

Chapter 1

A Growing Area of Litigation

'An action for negligence against a doctor is for him unto a dagger.
His professional reputation is as dear to him as his body, perhaps
more so, and an action for negligence can wound his reputation as
severely as a dagger can his body.'

Since 1954, when Lord Denning used these words in the course of his
address to the jury in the case of *Hatcher* v *Black*,[1] thousands of daggers
have been aimed at medical and dental practitioners. The majority
have missed their mark and frequently it has been evident, in retrospect, that the initial assault had no chance of overcoming the formid-
able defences which the law has provided for both professions. Those
defences are not necessarily available to every other profession, as
was shown by Lord Mayfield's comments in *McRae* v *Henderson*.[2]

Defence societies—origins
Few areas of litigation have seen in recent years a larger and more
rapid increase in volume than actions alleging medical negligence.
Although there were cases last century of patients suing their medical
advisers, such was their rarity that in 1901, in *Farquhar* v *Murray*,[3] Lord
Young commented that for him the proceedings were unusual and
that, in all his experience, he had never seen a claim for damages
pursued against a doctor. It is evident, however, that claims, even in
very small numbers, were being made around this time. Within two
years, there came into existence the three defence societies which to
this day continue to protect and indemnify many doctors and dentists:
the Medical Defence Union (MDU), the Medical Protection Society
(MPS) and the Medical and Dental Defence Union of Scotland
(MDDUS).

At first their workload, so far as claims alleging negligence were
concerned, remained light. Even at the start of the second half of this
century there were few contested claims and fewer reported decisions
in Scotland. There was therefore a major gap in Scots law until the

[1] [1954] CLY 2289.
[2] 1989 SLT 523.
[3] (1901) 3F 859 at p 862.

1

1955 ruling in *Hunter* v *Hanley*,[4] a decision which remains the foundation of medical negligence law both in Scotland and elsewhere.

'Medical negligence'—the need for clarity

Prior to *Hunter* v *Hanley* there had not been a definitive ruling by a Scottish court of what constituted 'medical negligence'. In his supporting judgment Lord Sorn commented:

> 'It is curious that there should be no reported case in Scotland in which a decision had been given as to the grounds on which a doctor can be made liable in damages.'[5]

Until then it had been widely believed that nothing short of 'gross negligence' would do, and that was the basis on which Lord Patrick had charged the jury at the initial trial. The position, however, as to what standard of negligence a Scottish court would apply was anything but clear. In 1948 in *Crawford* v *Campbell*[6] Lord Blades appeared to approve the test of 'gross negligence' set out in *Farquhar* v *Murray*, while at the same time noting the ruling which prevailed in England in the case of *R* v *Bateman*.[7]

The views of Hewart CJ in *R* v *Bateman* that the law required 'a fair and reasonable standard of care and competence'[8] were contained in a judgment given in a criminal appeal. The case arose out of the death of a woman during a complicated delivery and Dr Bateman was successful in having his conviction for manslaughter quashed, along with a six-month prison sentence. As the Appeal Court's primary aim had been to deal with an important aspect of English criminal law, the Lord Chief Justice's views on questions of civil liability were largely *obiter dicta*. The judges had to decide whether a crime could be inferred if a woman died in labour and it was believed that the obstetrician had blundered.

The opinions expressed on civil liability were irrelevant to the decision on the manslaughter charge and Lord Blades's comment that 'The civil liability of a medical man towards his patient [was] defined by Lord Hewart CJ [in *R* v *Bateman*]'[9] does not appear to have taken into consideration the tragic circumstances of the particular case, nor that the view on which he founded was expressed in a criminal case.

The attitude which a Scottish court should adopt to an action averring medical negligence was further confused in 1954 by Lord Guthrie's allowance of a proof before answer in *Kenyon* v *Bell*.[10] In that case the pursuer based his claim on an allegation that the doctor 'had

---

[4] 1955 SC 200; 1955 SLT 213.
[5] Ibid, p 207.
[6] 1948 SLT (Notes) 91.
[7] [1925] All ER 45.
[8] Ibid, p 48.
[9] 1948 SLT (Notes) 91.
[10] 1953 SC 125; Outer House, unreported, 9th April 1954.

failed to exercise reasonable care and professional skill'—a vastly less onerous test than that he had been 'grossly negligent'. There was thus an overwhelming need for clarity; the decision in *Hunter* v *Hanley* provided it.

Hunter v *Hanley*—'medical negligence' defined

The landmark judgment, recognising that medicine and dentistry embrace a wide range of opinions and approaches, indicated that a mere difference of view or standard would not suffice. Dealing first with the need for an authoritative definition of what does or does not constitute medical negligence, the First Division of the Court of Session, through the words of Lord President Clyde, adopted a passage in *Glegg on Reparation*[11] and ruled:

> 'In the realm of diagnosis and treatment there is ample scope for genuine difference of opinion and one man clearly is not negligent merely because his conclusion differs from that of other professional men nor because he has displayed less skill or knowledge than others would have shown. The true test for establishing negligence in diagnosis or treatment on the part of a doctor is whether he has been proved to be guilty of such a failure as no doctor of ordinary skill would be guilty of if acting with ordinary care.'[12]

Later in the same judgment the court dealt with the extent to which a potential pursuer will require to go if a deviation from normal practice is to be the foundation of the action. In the penultimate paragraph of his judgment Lord President Clyde laid down the tests which have to be satisfied before a Scottish court will conclude that there has been negligence in such circumstances; for in his opinion it would be 'disastrous' if deviations from ordinary professional practice were regarded necessarily as evidence of negligence.

> 'Even a substantial deviation from normal practice may be warranted by the particular circumstances.'[13]

He then laid down the three tests or requirements which are needed to show medical negligence if a deviation or departure from usual practice is averred:

(1) There must be a usual and normal practice.
(2) It must be proved that the doctor or dentist did not follow that practice.
(3) '[I]t must be established that the course . . . adopted is one which no [doctor or dentist] of ordinary skill would have taken if he had been acting with ordinary care.'

[11] 3rd edn, p 509.
[12] 1955 SC 200 at p 204–205.
[13] Ibid, p 206.

3

Attempts to extend the need to satisfy those three stringent requirements to every case of alleged professional negligence have been
rejected by the courts; accordingly, medical and dental practitioners
have been placed in a special position so far as any claim suggesting
negligence based on a different practice or procedure is concerned.

The terms of *Hunter* v *Hanley* and the tests propounded in it were
summarised in *Phillips* v *Grampian Health Board*.[14] In his judgment in
that case Lord Clyde stated that the obligation on a pursuer was that:

> '[He] must prove that there was such an error as no doctor of
> ordinary skill would be guilty if he were acting with reasonable
> care.'

The three tests are referred to in more detail in chapter 3.

Duty of care

Attempts to avoid liability by suggesting that there was no contract
between the doctor and the patient floundered as long ago as 1914
when in *Edgar* v *Lamont*[15] a defence on those grounds was rejected.
That case and the earlier one of *Lanphier* v *Phipos*[16] date from a time
when society did not accord women equal rights and a husband
entered into contracts for his spouse. As the right to damages and the
measure of them could vary considerably depending on whether
the action was based on delict or contract, the decision in *Edgar* v
Lamont was of some significance, particularly when the alleged
injury was restricted to pain and suffering and no actual loss could be
proved.

The action arose out of the alleged failure of a doctor to treat
properly a cut finger which Mrs Edgar had suffered. Ultimately the
finger was amputated and Mrs Edgar raised proceedings. The doctor
pled that his contract was with the husband, as Mrs Edgar, a married
lady, had no ability to contract a debt for the doctor's fee. He invited
the court to find that she had no title to sue.

Both the Lord Ordinary and the Inner House judges rejected the
defender's argument. Referring to a number of English cases, Lord
Salvesen indicated that the law in Scotland was similar in allowing
a patient a right of action *ex delicto* against a doctor for professional
negligence. He concluded:

> 'To hold otherwise would lead to an entire denial of any remedy to
> a person who did not happen to be the person who had contracted
> with the doctor, and I should be very slow to arrive at that result.
> It seems to me that the clear ground of action is that a doctor owes
> a duty to the patient, whoever has called him in and whoever is
> liable for his bill, and it is for breach of that duty that he is liable, in

[14] (OH) 1991 SCLR 817; [1991] 3 Med LR 16; 1992 SLT 659.
[15] 1914 SC 277.
[16] (1838) 8 C & P 475.

other words, that it is for negligence arising in the course of the employment, and not in respect of breach of contract with the employer.'[17]

It is possible to sue on the basis of contract if an agreement or undertaking exists, as it may do for a private patient. Lord Wheatley posed the possibility in his dissenting judgment in *Robertson* v *Bannigan*[18] when he opined that *Hunter* v *Hanley* was a case in which a contractual position had existed, although the action was contested as a delictual one. With the growth in the number of cases of cosmetic surgery at private clinics, there appears to be no reason why a dissatisfied patient should not try the breach-of-contract route through the courts. Whether the action will succeed will depend on the facts and the exact terms of the agreement or promise.

Increase in number and value of claims

After *Hunter* v *Hanley* the growth in the number of claims made against health boards and the three defence societies was initially slow, and the increase was merely steady until the early 1980s, but there has undoubtedly been a massive rise in the last 10 years. The figures for Scotland show that between 1987 and 1995 there was a fourfold increase in the number of claims made against general practitioners and that the claims against dentists rose by 150 per cent.[19]

Along with the rise in the number of claims, there has been a spectacular rise in the sums sued for and awarded. Many patients, who in the past would probably have died following a medical blunder, now, owing to advances in resuscitation, survive. They may, however, be left permanently disabled or even brain damaged and as a consequence need a great deal of help and nursing assistance. This inevitably results in a far larger award than would have been the case if the claim had merely been that of a relative seeking solatium and loss of support.

Why there has been such a dramatic increase in the number of claims is difficult to explain. Patients are undoubtedly more conscious of their rights, and the publicity given to certain successful actions may also have contributed. The availability of legal aid is another factor (although a sizeable personal contribution can be a deterrent). There is no evidence that today's doctors and dentists have become more careless or are making more mistakes than their predecessors. The two professions continually review and upgrade their standards, and both the General Medical Council (GMC) and the General Dental Council (GDC) enforce them with far more vigour and power than used to be the case. The answer to the question as to why there has been a

[17] 1914 SC 277 at p 279–280.
[18] 1965 SLT 66.
[19] MDDUS Claims Records, 1987–1996.

mushrooming of claims probably lies in a rise in the public's perceptions and expectations.

Indemnity

Throughout this century until 1990 doctors and dentists looked to one of the three defence societies for indemnity against claims arising out of their work. Membership was compulsory for every practitioner employed by a health authority, including all hospital doctors, and the extent of the annual subscription and any increase was a factor included by the Department of Health in assessing the rates of doctors' and dentists' pay.

The Medical Defence Union (MDU) and the Medical Protection Society (MPS) are based in London (although each now has an office in the north of England). Accordingly they have comparatively few members in Scotland. Most practitioners north of the border belong to the Medical and Dental Defence Union of Scotland (MDDUS) which is based in Glasgow and recruits its membership largely from the graduates of the four medical and two dental schools in the Scottish universities. The MDDUS also offers membership to graduates of other universities in either of the disciplines.

The defence societies work closely together and this has enabled them to build up an immense depth of experience and knowledge. One of their primary aims is to protect the reputation of each of their members. This can result in a totally different approach from that adopted by an insurance company, to whom an economic settlement may have more appeal. As was shown by the opinions in *Medical Defence Union Ltd* v *Department of Trade*,[20] the three societies are not insurance companies but friendly societies, founded and continued for the protection of their members and not solely as indemnity agencies. They can and do fight cases on principle, and litigants who have hoped for an *ex gratia* payment or a compromise settlement have, on occasion, been disappointed.

In January 1990, because of the size of a series of claims in England and Wales relating to a number of brain-damaged children, it was decided that certain doctors throughout the United Kingdom should be given 'Crown indemnity'.[21] From the beginning of that month all National Health Service (NHS) hospital doctors came under the umbrella protection given to other employees of health boards and no longer needed separate insurance cover. After that date any action alleging negligence by a hospital doctor arising out of his NHS work in the hospital became the sole responsibility of the health authorities. Many practitioners, however, continue their defence society membership so that they can be separately and independently represented at any fatal accident inquiry or internal investigation.

[20] [1979] 2 WLR 686.
[21] NHS Circular 1989 (PCS/32).

It should be noted in passing that the protection given to the Crown, as the result of which it was impossible to sue the Crown as employer of a doctor or dentist working as a member of the Armed Services, ended on 15th May 1987. On that date the relevant parts of the National Health Service (Amendment) Act 1986 and the Crown Proceedings (Armed Forces) Act 1987 came into effect.

Vicarious liability and the NHS

With the creation of the NHS in 1948, although there was a legal obligation on each health board or authority to accept vicarious liability for any doctor working in any of its hospitals it was possible to seek recompense from the relevant defence society. This was in terms of a Government Circular[22] which recognised the independence of the medical profession and whose terms, although later revised, acknowledged the need to treat hospital doctors differently from other employees of the state-run health service. A special arrangement existed for the payment of expenses and the cost of fighting cases where the board was the only defender, but any liability was totally medical.

Prior to the implementation of the National Health Service (Scotland) Act 1947, doctors who worked in a hospital were regarded as being independent of the hospital's board of management, and accordingly vicarious liability did not arise. The decisions in *Lavelle* v *Glasgow Royal Infirmary*[23] and *Reidford* v *Aberdeen Magistrates*[24] supported the view that the governing body of a public hospital were not responsible 'for the negligent discharge of their professional duties by competent doctors'. The creation of a unified NHS, however, changed the position and in *Macdonald* v *Glasgow Western Hospitals Board of Management*[25] the Scottish courts agreed that vicarious liability did arise.

Earlier attempts to argue that the 1947 Act intended to exclude liability for any claim of medical negligence made against a board for the actings of a doctor or surgeon had been rebuffed by the courts. Section 70 provided that a board of management 'shall not be liable for any irregularity committed by their officers in execution of [s 166 of the Public Health (Scotland) Act 1897]'. It was argued in a number of legal debates that the word 'irregularity' included negligence, and that therefore any claim based on the alleged fault of an employee was incompetent. The argument went far beyond questions arising out of possible medical negligence and extended, for example, to whether a board could be liable for a claim when a female employee injured her hand while operating a roller in a hospital laundry. In

[22] NHS Circular 1954 (Hm/32).
[23] 1932 SC 245; 1932 SLT 179.
[24] 1933 SC 276; 1933 SLT 155.
[25] 1954 SC 453; 1954 SLT 226.

McGinty v *Glasgow Victoria Hospitals Board*[26] the judges held that 'irregularity' did not have an extended meaning to include acts of negligence.

This confirmed the opinion given by Lord Strachan in the earlier case of *Davis's Tutor* v *Glasgow Victoria Hospitals Board*.[27] That action, which arose out of a burning injury suffered by a child in the course of an operation to remove tonsils, was resisted on a number of grounds. Among these was the argument that the board were exempt from such a claim (alleging negligence by a nurse). Although the defenders were successful on other grounds, the judge rejected the attempt to argue a restrictive interpretation of the statute.

The line taken by Lord Strachan in *Davis's Tutor* v *Glasgow Victoria Hospitals Board* was confirmed in an appeal taken against the same judge's decision in *Macdonald* v *Glasgow Western Hospitals Board of Management*,[28] when he repeated the view he had expressed in *Davis's Tutor*. The case of *Macdonald* and that of *Hayward* v *Edinburgh Royal Infirmary Board of Management*,[29] which were conjoined for the appeal hearing, arose from allegations of negligence against certain doctors. Lord President Cooper summarised the court's view when he stated:

> 'I find it quite impossible to read the statutory provisions for the new Health Services Scheme as if the only duty imposed on the Hospital Board was an administrative one, involving merely that the Board should introduce the patient to the hospital medical personnel and to leave them to do their best, however negligently, without further responsibility on the Board, other than the responsibility "to provide an efficient, heated, clean and wholesome sick-house, equipped with the necessary furniture and fittings . . . and to employ a competent staff". That may or may not have been the limited obligation incumbent on the old charitable voluntary hospital . . . it is not my conception of the duties imposed on the State hospitals which now enjoy a monopoly of hospital services.'[30]

He concluded:

> '[P]ersons in the position of the resident medical officers charged with negligence . . . are persons for whose negligence in the discharge of their professional work the Board must now accept responsibility.'[31]

Crown indemnity and the health boards

The effect of the 1990 change, making any allegation of professional negligence against a hospital doctor the sole responsibility of the

[26] 1951 SC 200; 1951 SLT 92.
[27] 1950 SC 382; 1950 SLT 392.
[28] 1954 SC 453 at p 457.
[29] 1954 SC 453; 1954 SLT 226.
[30] 1954 SC 453 at p 478.
[31] Ibid, p 479.

health board, can be of benefit to a potential pursuer. In the past it was sometimes necessary to specify whether blame was being attributed to the surgeon or the theatre nurse for a forgotten swab or a misplaced piece of surgical equipment; nowadays doctor and nurse are regarded as fellow employees for whom the health board have equal responsibility. It no longer matters to the board who was at fault between the two. In theory this should speed up the settlement of claims where liability is obvious, there no longer being any need to apportion blame between the health board (for the nurse) and the defence society (for the doctor).

The situation was even more complicated when more than one doctor was criticised, thereby perhaps involving two or even all three defence societies in the negotiations behind the scenes to apportion liability and the share of any damages. While these discussions continued, the pursuer and his advisers required to wait patiently.

The change on 1st January 1990 affected all claims, even those which were ongoing. It is now irrelevant when the claim arose or when proceedings commenced; the health boards require to indemnify fully all their employees, including doctors and dentists. Most boards continue to use the Central Legal Office in Edinburgh to handle claims and court cases on their behalf. Each of the defence societies has always had separate legal advice and representation. In the case of the MDU the same firm of London solicitors has undertaken the task for more than a hundred years.

The introduction of health trusts as part of the NHS does not affect the position. The health board or trust is vicariously responsible for the actings and omissions of its employees, including all doctors. Accordingly, every medical and dental practitioner working in an NHS hospital, be he a consultant or a houseman, is now covered by his board or trust for any claim arising out of his NHS work in the hospital, in the same way as any other employee.

'Independent contractors'
The health boards are, however, responsible only for the blunders of their employees and only for those that occur in the course of that employment. Private work done by doctors outside their NHS contract is not covered. This includes fee-earning work carried out for the NHS in a private hospital or clinic when there is a purge on waiting lists. A medical practitioner who provides emergency treatment at an accident while 'off duty' is probably not covered. In these cases any liability will rest with the doctor himself, and for that reason many hospital practitioners have elected to continue with their defence society membership.

The two most obvious groups not covered by Crown indemnity are general practitioners and dentists (other than those working full time in hospitals). Almost all GPs and some dentists practise under the

NHS, but they are not employees of the health boards. Although each local health board retain certain responsibilities for GPs and dentists and have an overall duty to regulate and control the provision of all medical and dental services under the NHS in their area, they have no legal liability for the faults or errors of GPs or dentists.

In *Bonthrone* v *Secretary of State for Scotland*[32] the parents of a brain-damaged child sought to blame the family GP and the health visitor. They claimed that their child's condition followed the administration of a whooping-cough vaccination. They sought damages from the health board, claiming that they were vicariously responsible for both the GP and the health visitor. After a legal debate it was held that although the board were liable for any negligent act by the health visitor, they had no responsibility for the GP. At the subsequent proof all the defenders were assoilzied.

A health board cannot therefore be sued for any alleged negligence by an 'independent contractor'. All GPs and dentists (other than full-time hospital appointees) are 'independent contractors' and all (except the very foolish or irresponsible) are members of one of the defence societies, which continue to provide them with indemnity cover. Thus a claim against a GP or a family dentist must be raised against a named individual.

The normal rules and responsibilities arising out of partnership apply equally to doctors and dentists. It is therefore possible to sue all members of a GP practice in an attempt to recover damages following the negligence of one partner. It is, however, essential to differentiate between the situation where a number of doctors use the same health centre and may even share a receptionist (but are independent of each other) and one where there is a formal partnership. There is a growing tendency for different GP groups to share responsibility for night calls; that, like shared premises or staff, would not create a partnership.

[32] 1987 SLT 34.

Chapter 2

FAULT, LOSS AND A
BREACHED DUTY OF CARE

As with any other personal injuries action, anybody who can prove fault, loss and a breached duty of care can endeavour to recover damages. In *Hamilton* v *Fife Health Board*[1] the question of whether a claim could arise if an unborn child was injured and died from those injuries shortly after birth was considered. The Extra Division supported the views expressed in *McWilliams* v *Lord Advocate*[2] and concluded that (a) 'a child *in utero* does not have the legal status of being a person' (per Lord Caplan)[3] and (b) 'personal injuries' within the meaning of s 1(1) of the Damages (Scotland) Act 1976 include 'injuries inflicted to the person of the child immediately before his birth and continuing to have their effect on him by impairing his physical condition at and after the time of his birth' (per Lord McCluskey).[4]

Risk of failure

Neither medicine nor dentistry is an exact science and mishaps and accidents can occur without giving rise to a claim for negligence. It has long been accepted that certain procedures carry with them a risk of failure or complications, and unforeseen problems can also arise. The result can be scars or unsightly marks following cosmetic surgery or attempts to remove tattoos, failed sterilisations, adverse reactions to dental anaesthesia or intravenous sedation, an inability to achieve a perfect diagnosis from an X-ray, and a fractured jaw following attempts to remove a wisdom tooth.

Doctors and dentists are to some extent victims of their own legends. Many people appear to believe that almost anything can be achieved by a skilled practitioner, and when the desired result does not follow, complaints are made and the question of whether or not to sue can arise.

[1] (OH) 1992 SCLR 288; 1993 SLT 624.
[2] (OH) 1992 SCLR 954; 1992 SLT 1045.
[3] 1993 SLT 624 at p 630.
[4] Ibid, p 629.

Removal of tattoos and cosmetic surgery
It is recognised within the profession that the removal of tattoos without leaving scars or marks is virtually impossible. Provided the patient has been warned of this, and no promise or guarantee of success has been made, it is unlikely that there will be any valid claim for damages. Only if the residual scarring is far in excess of what is normal, and it can be shown that it is due to erroneous or incompetent treatment, would a right of action exist.

The same applies to cosmetic surgery, where success is often limited and a patient's hopes and expectations may be in excess of reality. Mere failure to achieve a total transformation will not, on its own, be accepted by the courts as proof of negligence. If, however, a promise or guarantee was given, then, depending on its terms, an action for breach of contract could arise.

Failed sterilisation
In the same way that a cosmetic operation which is only partly successful is not *per se* evidence of negligence, so a failed sterilisation does not automatically mean that the surgeon has fallen below the requisite standard of care. The operation can take various forms and some have a recognised, if slight, failure rate where, for instance, natural growth reconnects a severed tube or rings on fallopian tubes become displaced. Negligence could arise if there was a failure to remove an adequate portion of tube to limit the chances of natural regeneration, if too few rings were used, or if they were misplaced. The relevant element would require to be proved; the mere failure of the operation would not be sufficient.

Dental treatment
Every year a tiny number of people die, for no apparent reason, while undergoing a general dental anaesthetic. Research and expert opinion have failed to come up with a complete explanation. Terror or a bad dream have been suggested as possible causes. What is clear is that a death in the dentist's chair is not *per se* evidence of a negligent act or omission. Health boards and the defence societies can point to cases where every possible precaution was taken, the equipment used was in perfect order and where, despite all that, a catastrophe occurred. Because of the recognised risks, it is no longer permissible for a dentist to carry out his own general anaesthesia. Anybody who does so in normal circumstances will probably face a criminal prosecution and will undoubtedly be struck off by the General Dental Council. As well as requiring a qualified anaesthetist to be in attendance, modern practice expect up-to-date equipment, including everything necessary for on-the-spot resuscitation; yet apparently healthy people die without it being possible to determine the cause, let alone to lay the blame at anybody's door.

Some dentists use intravenous sedation in their work. Occasionally a patient suffers an adverse reaction to the particular drug used, but again this does not always mean that there has been negligence. Provided a full medical history has been sought and there is no reason to anticipate an allergic response, the basis of a successful claim does not exist. It is another instance of the body reacting in a way which defies explanation and where a problem cannot be anticipated.

In a number of instances claims have been made where a mandible was fractured following an attempt to extract a back tooth. The force required to remove certain teeth can be considerable and this has occasionally resulted in a broken jaw. This is not necessarily an obvious case of a lack of adequate care by the dentist. It is a recognised hazard of the procedure, even when carried out with the minimum of force and the greatest possible skill.

Similarly, if a dentist, while endeavouring to extract a tooth, ends up with a stump or part of a root still *in situ*, that does not necessarily indicate negligence. Unless it can be proved that the practitioner used the wrong technique, failed to carry out the appropriate preparation or applied excessive force, a claim will fail. Even the most careful dental expert sometimes experiences such misfortunes. As with any claim, it is for the pursuer to show negligence, not for the doctor or dentist to prove that the result was an unfortunate accident.

What, however, may give rise to a successful claim is if the dentist did not X-ray the jaw before starting or ignored an evident problem if an X-ray was taken. To fail to ascertain the exact position of the tooth roots or to proceed in the face of an apparent danger could give rise to a damages award if there is a subsequent problem. The fault would lie in not carrying out the appropriate preparation to ensure that the maximum information was available before proceeding, rather than in the operation itself.

It would still be necessary for a pursuer to prove not only that the dentist had failed to carry out the appropriate steps, but also that, had he done so, the injury would have been avoided. Accordingly, if the patient's tooth would have disintegrated even if reasonable force had been used, or if the jaw would have been damaged anyway, then although it will be possible to prove negligence, it will be equally impossible to show a loss arising therefrom. A number of claims, both medical and dental, fail because they are unable to clear this second hurdle.

It would, of course, be possible to argue that excessive force had been used and that that was the cause of the catastrophe, but such a case would be very difficult to prove. A dentist faced with such a claim could refer to a number of dental histories showing that, even in the best surgeries, a fracture can occur without there being any evidence of excessive pressure.

In the unreported case of *Warner* v *Payne*[5] Goddard J (as he then was) refused to accept that, simply because Mrs Warner's jaw had been fractured in the course of an extraction, liability followed automatically. In his judgment he concluded:

> 'I think that both the plaintiff and her husband had in mind all along that, provided they could prove that there was a fracture, or that the fracture was caused in the extraction of the tooth, they had a just ground for complaint against the dentist. I should certainly not hold that the mere fact that the jaw was fractured in the course of an extraction would be of itself any evidence of negligence against the dentist at all.'

That view was supported in the later case *Fish* v *Kapur*.[6] In that case Mrs Fish unsuccessfully sought damages after her jaw was fractured when Mr Kapur was attempting to extract her bottom-right wisdom tooth. Not only was her jaw fractured, the dentist left part of the root of the tooth behind. Expert evidence showed that neither misfortune was, *per se*, proof of negligence and that each was a recognised hazard of the procedure.

Agreeing that Goddard J had correctly stated the law in *Warner* v *Payne*, Lynskey J added:

> 'I cannot hold that because a fracture was caused in the process of extraction of a tooth it was in itself any proof of negligence.'[7]

X-rays
With regard to X-rays it should be borne in mind that even the most experienced consultant radiologist may not be able to pinpoint a source of trouble in its early stages. The position of other bony structures can make it difficult to get to a clear enough view to make a definite decision. A mistake in reading an X-ray is not automatically negligent. In retrospect, and in the light of later developments or a subsequent X-ray, it may be possible to see vague pointers to the ultimate and correct diagnosis, but a court will look at it from the point of view of somebody who does not have second sight and who has to make a judgment in a busy department while reviewing a large number of films.

In *Doherty* v *British Telecommunications plc*,[8] a medical negligence case, there were contrary views as to whether there had been a failure to interpret certain X-rays. There were also differing opinions as to what treatment should be undertaken if the exact condition was known. The court refused to find that there had been negligence or that the outcome would necessarily have differed.

---

[5] 15th April 1935, quoted in *Fish* v *Kapur*, below.
[6] [1948] 2 All ER 176.
[7] Ibid, p 178.
[8] 1993 GWD 32-2069.

The onus of proof
It is important to specify exactly what action or omission any claim is based upon and in particular it is necessary to realise that the doctrine of *res ipsa loquitur* does not automatically apply to every case in the world of medical negligence. Attempts to invoke it in certain negligence cases have met with only limited success. In *Dwyer* v *Roderick*[9] May LJ rejected an argument founded upon that legal presumption stating 'I do not think that such a plea (is) apt'. A similar argument, although not formally based on the principle, equally failed before the House of Lords in the tragic case of *Kay's Tutor* v *Ayrshire and Arran Health Board*.[10]

One occasion on which the doctrine was accepted was in *Clarke* v *Worboys*,[11] where the patient was found to have a severe burn after she had received treatment which included the passing of an electrical current through a pad attached to a buttock.

Unless and until this country has a scheme of no fault compensation (New Zealand, where such a scheme has been in existence for many years, has experienced considerable problems, particularly in the field of medical mishaps), there will always be a number of sad and difficult cases where no compensation is due.

One such case was *Ingrams* v *Ritchie*.[12] Mrs Ingrams sustained a debilitating stroke six days after being prescribed 'the pill' by her GP. She was unable to prove that there was a causal connection between the illness and the medication. It was, however, accepted that in certain cases the risk of a complication is increased if the patient is a smoker. Mrs Ingrams was a heavy smoker and she argued that Dr Ritchie should have avoided prescribing such a drug which for her had those extra risks. That head of claim was rejected also.

Establishing a causal connection
As with any claim for delict, it is necessary to prove not only that there has been negligence but that that negligence is the cause of the loss or suffering on which the claim is based. Even where negligence is obvious and admitted, it is sometimes impossible to prove a causal connection between the *culpa* and the patient's subsequent condition.

This was illustrated in *Kay's Tutor* v *Ayrshire and Arran Health Board*.[13] A young child suffering from meningitis was correctly prescribed penicillin. Unfortunately, while in hospital, he was given a grossly excessive dose of the drug and suffered convulsions. He later developed paralysis on one side of his body, although, like the convulsions,

[9] *The Times*, 12th November 1983.
[10] 1987 SC (HL) 145; 1987 SLT 577.
[11] [1952] CLY 2443; *The Times*, 18th March 1952.
[12] 1989 GWD 27-1217.
[13] See note 10 above and 1988 SLT (News) 25.

this was only temporary. Subsequently the child became profoundly deaf, a condition for which there was no cure.

Mr Kay sued the board on behalf of his son. He claimed that, owing to the dosage error, not only had the boy suffered convulsions and the temporary paralysis, the deafness had its root cause in the same blunder. He sought damages to include a large amount to compensate for this. It was, however, impossible to show that the ultimate outcome was caused by the penicillin overdose; on the contrary, the court heard a substantial body of expert opinion to the effect that the overdose had merely caused a temporary problem, and that the child's deafness was entirely due to the initial illness. Damages were accordingly limited to solatium for the period while the effects of the overdose caused additional, if transient, suffering.

In *Kenyon* v *Bell*[14] the pursuer, a father suing on behalf of his daughter, succeeded in showing that the doctor had been negligent but failed to recover damages because the judge concluded that the child would have lost her eye anyway as the result of the initial accident which gave rise to the request for medical treatment. Although the final judgment is unreported, the outcome was envisaged by the defender at the earlier procedure hearing[15] before Lord Guthrie. At that stage an application by the pursuer for a jury trial was successfully opposed.

Another case which illustrates the difficulties which can arise in trying to pursue a claim to a successful conclusion is *Bolitho* v *City and Hackney Health Authority*.[16] A doctor failed to respond to two urgent calls to attend a two-year-old with acute breathing difficulties. It was established that had the doctor attended in response to the calls and had she intubated the child on her arrival, the child would not have died. It was accepted that the doctor had been negligent in failing to attend. There was, however a dispute as to what she would have done if she had come in response to either summons. There were competing theories in the medical profession as to the desirability of intubating *in situ* in such circumstances and it was agreed that if intubation had not been undertaken on the spot, the child would not have survived. The crucial question on which the court had to be satisfied if the claim was to succeed was whether the doctor, assuming she had responded to the initial call, would have intubated the child before taking further steps. The plaintiff could not convince the judge that, on a balance of probabilities, the doctor would have undertaken the necessary procedure. As there was an acceptable body of medical opinion which backed a policy of delaying such action, it could not be said that a doctor who failed to intubate in such circumstances was negligent. The claim accordingly failed, despite the fact

[14] Outer House, unreported, 9th April 1954.
[15] 1953 SC 125.
[16] [1993] 4 Med LR 381.

that there was a negligent act (the failure to attend when an urgent call had been made) and that a child had died following the delay.

The need to prove that the outcome would have been different had the negligent act or omission not occurred is a stumbling block which prevents far more claims succeeding than is perhaps realised. It is, however, a potential difficulty which must not be overlooked.

The case of *Barnett* v *Chelsea and Kensington Hospital Management Committee*[17] illustrates how a clear case of negligence can still end with a claimant receiving nothing. The judge had no difficulty in concluding that a casualty house officer who failed completely to treat a night watchman who was suffering from the effects of arsenic poisoning was at fault. The man had drunk the fatal cocktail when his tea, together with that of two colleagues, became contaminated. There was, however, no effective antidote which could have been given by the time the patient reached the hospital three hours later. The court decided that the man would have died anyway and accordingly there was no loss which could be attributed to the negligent act.

Proving both negligence and loss

In certain respects a claim alleging medical negligence is no different from any claim for personal injury. The standard of proof required is on a balance of probabilities, and it is necessary to prove both a negligent act and a loss or injury which would not have occurred but for it. If the outcome would have been the same, or if it is impossible to show that the injury arose from the complained of act or neglect, the claim will fail. Both legs of the case must be satisfied and in assessing whether a valid claim exists, it is necessary to have sufficient evidence on both points.

Even when a court is satisfied that there has been a negligent act or omission, and the patient has suffered pain or even permanent disability, it may only be possible to attribute a part of that pain/ disability to the negligence. In *Purryag* v *Greater Glasgow Health Board*[18] Lord Abernethy held that even if he had found negligence proved, it was clear that most of the damage to the patient occurred before the doctor was advised of the problem. Having indicated what he would have awarded on full liability, the judge ruled that, had any sum been due, only 20 per cent could be attributed to events after the doctor's involvement started. In the event the pursuer failed to establish any head of claim (which arose out of complications during the pursuer's birth many years before) and the board and doctors were granted absolvitor.

Although the doctors were assoilzied in *Doherty* v *British Telecommunications plc*, the judge indicated that had he decided the issue of liability in the pursuer's favour, he would have limited any award to

[17] [1969] 1 QB 428. See also *Rance* v *Mid-Downs Health Authority* [1991] 1 All ER 801.
[18] 1996 GWD 10-584 (on merits); 1996 SLT 794 (on interest).

40 per cent of the full value. This would have been on the basis that the patient would have had certain pain and discomfort as the result of the original injury which led to the hospitalisation.

The normal rules and standards apply to the assessment of any damages. The appropriate solatium for the loss of a limb is exactly the same whether it was caused by a careless driver or a negligent doctor. If the court concludes that there has been negligence and that it has caused loss, it will assess the value of the claim using the same criteria.

Chapter 3

ESSENTIAL ELEMENTS OF A CLAIM

Some cases of medical negligence are obvious and require little research in order to establish a right of action. The amputation of the wrong limb, a gross miscalculation in a drug dosage, the extraction of incorrect teeth or a failure to investigate an obvious tumour—all, if they caused extra suffering or loss, would provide a sound basis for a successful case.

If it is possible to show that a dentist or doctor has subjected a patient to excessive and unnecessary treatment, that could give rise to a claim. It is sometimes, particularly with dental treatment, difficult to prove this. In the case of an allegation that a filling or course of treatment was totally unnecessary, the evidence of whether there ever was a problem has often been destroyed by the very work complained about. In such a situation the state of adjacent teeth or the practitioner's note may prove to be invaluable.

Professional judgment and opinion

Most medical negligence cases are, however, complex and often involve matters of professional judgment and opinion. Such was the situation in *Hunter* v *Hanley*,[1] the foundation of modern case-law north and south of the border. Although as early as 1901 in *Farquhar* v *Murray*[2] a Scottish court had required to deal with an action based on an allegation of medical negligence, the decision turned, as Lord President Clyde pointed out in *Hunter*, 'wholly on its [own] facts'. The field was therefore clear for Lord Clyde and his colleagues to lay down the factors needed in a medical negligence suit and in particular in a case where a deviation from normal or usual practice is alleged.

In a passage which has been referred to ever since, the Lord President ruled:

> 'To establish liability by a doctor where deviation from normal practice is alleged, three facts require to be established. First of all it must be proved that there is a usual and normal practice.

[1] 1955 SC 200; 1955 SLT 213. See also '*Hunter* v *Hanley* 35 years on' 1990 SLT 325 and '*Hunter* v *Hanley* 35 years on: a reply' 1991 SLT 321.
[2] (1901) 3F 859.

Secondly it must be proved that the defender has not adopted that practice, and thirdly (and this is of crucial importance) it must be established that the course the doctor adopted is one which no professional man of ordinary skill would have taken if he had been acting with ordinary care. There is clearly a heavy onus on a pursuer to establish these three facts, and without all three his case will fail.'[3]

Subsequent cases have emphasised the fluid state of knowledge and practice in the fields of medicine and dentistry. In 1964, in the case of *Morrison Associated Companies Ltd* v *James Rome & Sons Ltd*,[4] Lord Cameron stated:

'The practice of medicine is not an exact science and methods of practice and treatment vary with the movement of professional opinion and the expansion of the horizon of scientific knowledge.'

A quarter of a century later his son, Lord Cameron of Lochbroom, made a similar point when, in *Goorkani* v *Tayside Health Board*,[5] he recalled Lord President Clyde's view that:

'In the realm of diagnosis and treatment there is ample scope for genuine difference of opinion and one man is clearly not negligent merely because his conclusion differs from that of other professional men.'

He then confirmed that, as had been pointed out in other cases averring professional negligence, 'Each case . . . must depend on its own peculiar circumstances', before reaching the conclusion that, on the particular facts of the case, medical negligence had been established.

Divergent professional opinions
Because the practice of medicine or dentistry is not an exact science, cases of alleged negligence often result in a clash of professional opinions, although in practice it may be merely a question of emphasis. In *Gordon* v *Wilson*[6] there was a clear divergence of views. The pursuer complained that her GP had been negligent in failing to diagnose a tumour at an early stage. As the result of the delay in referring her to a specialist, she averred that she had sustained nerve damage that would not have occurred if a timely diagnosis had been made. At the proof Lord Penrose heard the opinions of two experts. Both were of the view that it was a rare event for a GP to find a patient with a brain tumour and that, furthermore, only a small proportion of brain tumours turn out to be meningiomas (as was the situation with

[3] 1955 SC 200 at p 206.
[4] 1964 SC 160; 1964 SLT 249 at p 255.
[5] 1991 SLT 94 at p 95.
[6] 1992 SLT 849.

Mrs Gordon). Where the experts did not agree was in what the GP should have done when initially presented with his patient's complaints and having carried out a full examination (as it was agreed he had done). One was of the view that Dr Wilson should have made an urgent hospital appointment for Mrs Gordon to enable her to be seen by a specialist. The other expert (both were experienced GPs) stated that, in his opinion, an urgent referral, on the limited information available at the time, was not justified.

Lord Penrose found that both experts were 'men of wide experience' and that each had given 'evidence which was credible and reliable in the sense that each expressed opinions which he clearly honestly held and honourably represented in an accurate way'.[7] He concluded that this was a situation where

'there are two bodies of credible and reliable testimony which support differing opinions as to whether the course adopted was or was not in conformity with the standard required in the circumstances'.[8]

He stated that where a court was confronted with such a dilemma,

'defenders' counsel was correct in identifying the test in *Hunter* v *Hanley* as central to the issue of liability in cases relating to diagnosis and patient management'.[9]

As the evidence of the defenders' expert was accepted and it therefore could not be said that *no* GP would have acted as Dr Wilson did, the claim failed. It is, as Lord Penrose pointed out, possible to test the credibility and reliability of a professional expert in the same way as any other witness. Where a pursuer is unable to shake the standing of the other side's expert, then, as was shown in *Gordon* v *Wilson* there will be no liability.

A similar outcome occurred in *Brady* v *Brown*.[10] Where consultants of equal eminence give opposite views, it would be difficult, even if one side was preferred, to find that negligence had been proved.

Any doubt there may have been that a Scottish court might be willing to 'prefer' one set of experts where there was a conflict was dispelled by Lord Coulsfield in *Miller* v *Lanarkshire Health Board*.[11] Invited to consider the English decision of *Beswick* v *North Manchester Health Board Authority*,[12] he indicated that the approach adopted in that action, where the judge 'was less impressed by the experts led by [one side]', was unsatisfactory. The position in Scotland remains that expressed by the First Division in *Hunter* v *Hanley*.

[7] Ibid, p 852.
[8] Ibid.
[9] Ibid.
[10] 1988 GWD 28-1194.
[11] 1993 SLT 453.
[12] Unreported, 14th March 1989.

State of knowledge

In testing standards of practice it is essential to look at the state of knowledge and the views of the profession at the time of any alleged failure of duty rather than at the date of the proof. Courts have affirmed this on a number of occasions because, in the medical world, standards change and views alter, often quite rapidly.

This was clearly illustrated in *Moyes* v *Lothian Health Board*[13] when Lord Caplan heard evidence as to how the thinking and approach of medical practitioners had developed and moved with the passage of time. Although *Moyes* was decided on the issue of the reliability of the principal witnesses, the judge indicated that it was evident that, between 1982, the date of the operation, and 1989, when he heard the evidence in the case, there had been a marked change in doctors' views on the question of how far, if at all, it was necessary to advise a patient of certain risks which attached to a particular procedure. In 1982 the evidence showed that half of all doctors concerned would not, as a matter of policy, have told their patients of the slight risks involved. By 1989 a poll of medical practitioners involved in deciding if it was appropriate to forewarn each patient revealed that two-thirds would give details before seeking consent, and half of those would provide very full information. Lord Caplan emphasised, however, that he required to look to the standards of 1982 in assessing the evidence.

The *Hunter* v *Hanley* tests

The three tests elucidated in *Hunter* v *Hanley* form the bedrock on which any action for medical negligence in Scotland must be based. No Scottish judge has ever sought to challenge their force or effect, and in numerous cases Lord President Clyde's words have been reaffirmed as correctly reflecting the true position north of the border. As *Hunter* v *Hanley* was an Inner House decision, it would probably need a House of Lords judgment in a Scottish appeal to alter the situation. In 1984, when a point arose in an English case before five Law Lords, *Hunter* v *Hanley*, and in particular the three tests necessary to show medical negligence where there is an alleged deviation from usual and normal practice, was expressly approved.[14]

'Usual and normal practice'

The first of the requirements needed to establish a valid case is that there is a 'usual and normal practice'.[15] To prove this a pursuer must be able to lead evidence from another practitioner who should be from the same branch of medicine as the doctor whose actings are under attack. The practitioner should be able to speak to proper practice at

---

[13] 1990 SLT 444.
[14] *Maynard* v *West Midands Regional Health Authority* [1985] 1 All ER 635.
[15] 1955 SC 200 at p 206.

the relevant time and he should be able to comment on recent developments by having kept himself up to date with progress in the particular field of medicine. A witness failed to satisfy Lord Caplan in this regard in *Moyes* v *Lothian Health Board* and the judge refused to certify him (a retired professor) as an expert.

The most common trap into which a pursuer's advisers fall is, in failing to get an opinion from a similar branch of medicine. This was illustrated in *Scott* v *Highland Health Board*,[16] where the pursuer's claim was based on the failure of a consultant radiologist to diagnose from a series of X-rays a condition of the femur. It was accepted that he had seen and examined radiographs which showed the relevant bone structure but had failed to notice any evidence to justify alerting a surgeon to the true cause of the problem. In support of the pursuer's case two consultant orthopaedic surgeons gave evidence critical of the radiologist, stating, in effect, that the problem should have been observed. In response the defenders called a consultant radiologist to explain what could be expected from somebody practising in that branch of medicine and in that particular type of hospital. He concluded that there was no justification for the allegation of negligence. In assessing the evidence the judge, Lord Maxwell, commented:

> 'I attach importance to the fact that only one of the three, Dr Davidson, was a consultant radiologist. I think it would be unsafe to draw any inference in the defenders' favour from the fact that the pursuer's advisers could not or did not see fit to call a radiologist as a witness, and I certainly would not reject as valueless the evidence of consultant orthopaedic surgeons merely because they are not of precisely the same discipline as the second defender. Nevertheless, other things being equal, I consider that a generalist consulting radiologist is better placed than a consultant orthopaedic surgeon to say what another competent and diligent generalist consultant radiologist would or would not have done.'

Courts clearly have to determine what is the 'usual and normal practice' in the circumstances in which a doctor finds himself. No cottage hospital has the facilities of a major teaching infirmary, nor does a junior doctor have the experience or the expertise of a consultant or university professor. A doctor dealing with a roadside emergency cannot be expected to have all the facilities available to him which exist in a surgery or consulting room. The courts accept that there is a wide variability in facilities, circumstances, experience and expertise. To prove negligence successfully, evidence from witnesses able to speak to the appropriate experience and expertise is essential.

[16] Outer House, unreported, 29th January 1981.

23

In deciding what is the 'usual and normal practice', the expert must be in a position to comment on the actual circumstances, including what facilities were available and the depth of knowledge expected from the particular doctor or dentist. This was shown in *Craig* v *Glasgow Victoria and Leverndale Hospitals Board of Management*[17] and *Aird* v *Ramsay*.[18]

In the former case a man attended at a large hospital to enable a general surgeon to explore and investigate a swelling in his neck. It was thought that the cause of the problem was a cyst. In fact once the operation had started it became apparent that Mr Craig had an extremely rare complaint: a carotid body tumour. The surgeon removed it but the patient's carotid artery which lay next to the tumour was damaged and he was left with the symptoms of a stroke.

In his action alleging negligence against the surgeon's employers, he led evidence from a vascular surgeon who had access to unique facilities in a top hospital. The pursuer's expert criticised the general surgeon for the manner in which he had performed the operation. He accepted, however, he had never personally undertaken the procedure himself. The board relied on the evidence of other general surgeons who had carried out similar operations and who supported the course of action and the manner of the operation undertaken by the board's employee. Because they had actual experience of that particular operation and belonged to the same branch of the medical profession as the surgeon who had carried out the operation on Mr Craig, their evidence carried more weight than the more highly qualified, but less experienced, expert cited by the pursuer.

Aird v *Ramsay* arose out of a mishap in a dental surgery, when in the course of treatment a root-canal reamer fractured. Although Sheriff Presslie reached a view adverse to the pursuer on the basis of credibility and reliability, he also required to consider conflicting opinions from a dentist in general practice and a hospital consultant as to how such a situation should be tackled. Both accepted that a fractured reamer was a recognised hazard for which no blame could be attributed. They did not agree, however, as to whether a surgical operation should have been attempted as soon as possible.

The court followed the line taken by Lord Maxwell in *Scott* v *Highland Health Board*. Where opinion evidence is put before the court, it is preferable that the view comes from somebody with comparable experience and facilities. What might have occurred if Mrs Aird had had her misfortune in a dental hospital with all its equipment and expertise was not a reasonable way to assess what a dentist in his own surgery should have done. The evidence of the dentist in general practice was preferred as to the appropriate standard of care.

[17] Outer House, unreported, 1st December 1972.
[18] Glasgow Sheriff Court, unreported, 5th December 1984.

Practice not adopted

The second of the three tests propounded in *Hunter* v *Hanley*[19] requires the pursuer to establish that the doctor or dentist 'has not adopted that practice' (ie, the 'usual and normal practice' of the first test). This is often a question of fact, but to succeed a claimant must be able to prove not only the existence of the 'usual and normal practice' but also that the defender failed to follow it. A Scottish court will not presume that there has been such a failure merely because a 'usual and normal practice' has been proved and a mishap has occurred. It will always be necessary for the pursuer to show what the doctor did or did not do, and how that course of action (or inaction) differed from 'the usual and normal' practice.

In *Devaney* v *Greater Glasgow Health Board*[20] it was suggested that the doctor had used the wrong operating technique. The claim failed because the evidence showed that there was a divergence of opinion within the profession as to the correct procedure, and accordingly the second test in *Hunter* v *Hanley* had not been satisfied. It was also held that, in accordance with *Kelly* v *City of Edinburgh District Council*,[21] there is no onus on a defender to justify the technique used.

Mr Devaney had undergone an operation as a child to repair a congenital condition of the aorta. Thereafter he was regularly monitored until 1981, when he was 17, it was discovered that a further operation would be necessary. This arose because re-coarctation had taken place and the original problem of a substantially narrowed aorta had returned. An operation was essential to remedy the situation, but it was accepted that there were various possible procedures and techniques which a surgeon could follow.

During the operation the patient suffered a cardiac arrest and was left paraplegic. He sued the surgeon, claiming *inter alia* that the doctor had used the wrong technique. From the selection available the surgeon had used a procedure which was different from that which he normally favoured. He did so because of a perceived risk of infection and difficulties caused by adhesions from the earlier operation. The procedure used, however, had the known disadvantage of permanently dividing the subclavian artery which feeds the main blood supply to the left arm, the vertebral artery and the deep cervical arteries on the left side. Lord Sutherland stated:

> 'There are several techniques for dealing with a coarctation of the aorta, each of which has advantages and disadvantages.'

Having considered the various merits and demerits of the different choices, the judge found that a responsible doctor will react to what he finds during the course of a surgical procedure.

[19] 1955 SC 200 at p 206.
[20] 1987 GWD 6-96.
[21] 1983 SLT 593.

'It is accordingly clear that a surgeon has a number of options open to him and while he may have a technique of choice in ordinary cases he must be prepared to vary his technique in particular circumstances depending on what he finds at the operation.'

A reclaiming motion by the unsuccessful pursuer was ultimately dropped.

The professional man of ordinary skill acting with ordinary care
That third and final test needed to show medical negligence according to *Hunter* v *Hanley* is the requirement to establish

'that the course the doctor adopted is one which no professional man of ordinary skill would have taken if he had been acting with ordinary care'.

Lord President Clyde gave added emphasis to the test when he advised that it was 'of crucial importance'. It is undoubtedly the most difficult point on which to satisfy a court and numerous patients have found that they cannot even get legal aid to pursue a claim because of its rigid terms. Unless an applicant can produce an opinion from a suitably qualified expert in the necessary terms to satisfy all three legs of *Hunter* v *Hanley*, the application will inevitably be successfully opposed.

As was conceded by Lord Clyde, the decision in *Hunter* v *Hanley* imposes 'a heavy onus on a pursuer to establish these three facts', and, as he added, 'without all three [a claimant's] case will fail'. Anybody advising a potential pursuer should ensure that the expert or experts whose testimony is to be relied upon are aware of the stringent terms of *Hunter* v *Hanley* and that their testimony will satisfy all three tests and in particular the final one. The witness must be able to state unequivocally (a) that, in the circumstances of the case, he would not have acted as the defender did, and (b) that *no* doctor acting with ordinary care would have so acted.

The case of *Kelly* v *Lanarkshire Health Board*[22] illustrates the point. The pursuer had, following the diagnosis of a disc lesion by an orthopaedic surgeon, been admitted to hospital for bed rest, traction and sedation. The purpose of the treatment was to immobilise the upper half of Mrs Kelly's body while traction allowed the misplaced disc to return to its original position. While in hospital she developed a deep venous thrombosis (DVT) which left her with a permanent disability. She sued the board as the employer of the surgeon.

It was accepted that a DVT is a recognised hazard where a patient is immobilised, so the claim proceeded under two headings. First, it was suggested that it was not necessary to use traction to cure a slipped disc, and that if the patient had not been immobilised she

---

[22] Airdrie Sheriff Court, unreported, 6th September 1988.

would not have developed the thrombosis with its disastrous effect. Secondly, it was averred that assuming that bed rest and traction were appropriate, special precautions should have been taken, including extra physiotherapy, to minimise the chances of a DVT.

The board had little difficulty in dealing with the latter argument. A physiotherapist gave evidence that she had worked with the pursuer regularly, and she was able to produce her contemporaneous notes as well as the hospital records in support. There remained, however, the initial contention that the wrong treatment had been applied. Two consultant orthopaedic surgeons of similar standing and experience as the defenders' employee gave evidence that, faced with the task of deciding on the appropriate type of treatment in such a case, they would have followed the normal practice of treating the patient without using traction, thereby avoiding any question of immobilising her while confining her to bed for a protracted period. The pursuer's experts thus dealt with the first two *Hunter* v *Hanley* tests. They proved first, that there was a usual and normal practice and, secondly, that the surgeon had not followed it.

Where the claim failed was in the concession, which both experts had to make, that although neither of them would have tackled the patient's treatment in the manner selected, there was a recognised body of medical opinion which supported that line. The two agreed that other reputable surgeons would have acted in exactly the same way as the defenders' surgeon. It therefore could not be contended that *no* doctor would have used the treatment prescribed if faced with such circumstances and symptoms. As Lord President Clyde's third test had not been satisfied, the health board were successful in their defence; medical negligence was not established.

Where the testimony of the expert is opinion evidence, it may be necessary to remind him of the responsibility which a court imposes on him. The position was summarised by Lord President Cooper in *Davie* v *Magistrates of Edinburgh*.[23] Referring to expert witnesses, he said:

> 'Their duty is to furnish the judge or jury with the necessary scientific criteria for testing the accuracy of their conclusions, so as to enable the judge or jury to form their own independent judgment by the application of these criteria to the facts proved in evidence.'

As far as dental practice is concerned, it may be thought that because a dentist has obtained approval from the Dental Practice Board (DPB) for a particular type of treatment, he can, if necessary, call on the concurrence and support of another dentist. This is not necessarily so. The word 'approved' in this context merely means that the dentist is authorised by the DPB to proceed and that the reasonable costs

[23] 1953 SC 34 at p 40; 1953 SLT 54.

involved will be met. It does not mean that the DPB's adviser considers that it is either clinically appropriate or proper to carry out that type of treatment.

The position of the DPB can be compared with that of the Scottish Legal Aid Board (SLAB). The mere fact that SLAB issues a civil legal aid certificate does not mean that a solicitor could not be sued for negligence if he pursued the wrong defender, proceeded with an incompetent action or chose a forum which did not have jurisdiction.

Approval for *Hunter* v *Hanley* furth of Scotland

Two years after the Scottish court made its ruling in *Hunter* v *Hanley* an English court adopted the same approach in *Bolam* v *Friern Hospital Management Committee*.[24] In his address to the jury (an action for medical negligence remains one for which a jury trial can still be sought both in England and in the Court of Session), McNair J quoted from the leading judgment in *Hunter* v *Hanley*. He then added:

> '[W]here you get a situation which involves the use of some special skill or competence . . . the test . . . is the standard of the ordinary skilled man exercising and professing to have that skill. A man need not possess the highest expert skill; it is well-established law that it is sufficient if he exercises the ordinary skill of an ordinary competent man exercising that particular art.'

Thus did McNair J confirm that *Hunter* v *Hanley* correctly reflected the position in England.

Ten years later the tests expounded in *Hunter* v *Hanley* were adopted by the Privy Council in the case of *Chin Keow* v *Government of Malaysia*.[25]

After the decision in *Bolam* v *Friern Hospital Management Committee* the English courts referred occasionally to the tests in *Hunter* v *Hanley*, although the wording used by McNair J in *Bolam* was the more frequently quoted. In the House of Lords judgments in the 1981 case of *Whitehouse* v *Jordan*[26] the dicta in *Bolam* were expressly approved, while those in *Hunter* v *Hanley*, although they had been mentioned in the Court of Appeal,[27] were not referred to. The matter was rectified three years later when Lord Scarman, delivering his reasons for refusing the patient's appeal in *Maynard* v *West Midlands Regional Health Authority*,[28] opined: 'I do not think that the words of Lord President Clyde in *Hunter* v *Hanley* can be bettered.' He then quoted the passage listing the three requirements which *Hunter* v *Hanley* imposes on all would-be claimants.

[24] [1957] 1 WLR 582 at p 586.
[25] [1967] 1 WLR 813.
[26] [1981] 1 All ER 267.
[27] [1980] 1 All ER 650 (CA).
[28] [1985] 1 All ER 635.

The reason why the House of Lords chose not to comment on *Hunter* v *Hanley* in *Whitehouse* v *Jordan* was because they basically decided the case on its facts. The action arose from a complicated delivery which resulted in a severely damaged child. Although the original trial judge found in favour of the plaintiff, both a majority of the Appeal Court and all five members of the House of Lords disagreed with his interpretation of the evidence. They overturned the award of £100,000, concluding that negligence had not been established. It was not until the Law Lords came to decide *Maynard* v *West Midlands Regional Health Authority* that it was necessary for them to consider, in depth, how far English law would go in setting tests to be applied in cases of alleged deviation from normal practice and whether it would adopt completely the *Hunter* v *Hanley* approach.

Although there have been many claims alleging medical negligence in England since *Maynard* v *West Midlands Regional Health Authority*, Lord Scarman's opinion, wholeheartedly adopting *Hunter* v *Hanley*, remains a major authority to which a judge will turn before deciding whether an action can succeed before an English court.

The facts in *Maynard* v *West Midlands Regional Health Authority* illustrate well the type of dilemma which a court can face. Mrs Maynard, a West Indian, was believed to be suffering from a chest tuberculosis, although there was a possibility that, instead, she had Hodgkin's disease. The former, and more likely, diagnosis was not life threatening, whereas Hodgkin's disease is often fatal unless tackled in its early stages. Tests to clarify whether she merely had tuberculosis would have taken a number of weeks. By that time, if Mrs Maynard was indeed suffering from Hodgkin's disease, it would probably have been too late to save her life.

There was no inherent risk in the tests if properly carried out. The choice facing Mrs Maynard's medical team was whether to accept the more likely diagnosis and risk a fatal delay, or to subject her to an exploratory operation which would provide them with an immediate and definite answer as to what she was suffering from, and what the prognosis was. The operation carried a known, if very slight, risk that Mrs Maynard's vocal cords could be damaged irreparably.

The consultants decided to proceed with the operation and quickly ascertained that Mrs Maynard had developed tuberculosis, for which a relatively easy cure existed. So far as her initial complaint was concerned, she made a complete recovery. Unfortunately, although the operation was carried out to the highest possible standard, it caused damage to the vocal cords and Mrs Maynard was left with a permanent disability.

She sued the health board and the doctors, alleging that they had been negligent in undertaking the invasive procedure when there was a known (if slight) risk involved. She further argued that, in her particular case, there were additional pointers against performing

29

the operation on the grounds that it was unnecessary. It was recognised in the medical profession that West Indians are more susceptible to tuberculosis, and the chances that that was the cause of Mrs Maynard's symptoms were therefore greater than for other patients.

At the trial, Comyn J heard expert evidence from seven doctors. Five were called by the plaintiff and stated that it was wrong to have embarked on the operation in the face of the factors pointing towards what turned out to be the correct diagnosis. They argued that when there is a medically recognised risk of permanent damage in the procedure, a doctor should avoid it unless there is a greater chance that the most obvious reason for the symptoms is incorrect. In their view the normal and generally accepted way to deal with such a case as Mrs Maynard's is to await the results of the tests (or, alternatively, additional symptoms) before embarking on an operation which has a known risk factor.

Two equally qualified consultants expressed the contrary view. They stated that had they been required to make a decision on the information available before the operation, they would have followed the same course of action as took place. They would, after considering all the facts, including the possible side-effects, have carried out the operation with a view to ascertaining immediately the true cause of Mrs Maynard's illness.

In his written decision the judge indicated that, although he found all the witnesses credible and reliable, he 'preferred' the opinion of the five doctors called on behalf of the plaintiff and accordingly he found in her favour. The Court of Appeal reversed the decision, but only by a majority. Their reasons for doing so were varied and depended to some extent on a particular interpretation of the evidence. As it was a split decision and the issues raised appeared to be complex, there was no problem in the unsuccessful party obtaining leave to argue her case in the House of Lords before Lords Fraser, Elwyn-Jones, Scarman, Roskill and Templeman.

Lord Scarman, with whose views the other Lords of Appeal agreed, found that where a court was faced with two bodies of reputable medical opinion, it was not possible for a judge to conclude that medical negligence had been proved merely by his 'preferring' one line of thought to the other. In Lord Scarman's view, the crucial word in Lord President Clyde's opinion in *Hunter* v *Hanley* was 'no', where he stated that a claim based on an alleged deviation from normal practice could only succeed if the claimant established that it was a course which 'no professional man of ordinary skill would have taken if he had been acting with ordinary care'. In Mrs Maynard's case the trial judge heard expert opinion from two doctors, whose views he did not reject. These doctors supported the decision which was taken to proceed with the operation in the light of all the information available at the time. It therefore could not be said that *no* doctor would have acted as the claimant's medical advisers did. Two reputable medical practitioners gave evidence that they would have done likewise. An essential element for proving medical negligence was therefore missing; thus the action for damages failed.

There can be little doubt that Mrs Maynard would have fared no better had she been able to pursue her claim in Scotland. Lord Scarman's words brought English law, at least for that case, to the same point at which Scots law had been since 1955. Although the position has remained constant in Scotland and *Hunter* v *Hanley* continues to be accepted as the primary authority, the situation south of the border seems to be more fluid.

The facts and circumstances of *Maynard* v *West Midlands Regional Health Authority* illustrate as clearly as any the extent to which a court needs to go before it can find a doctor guilty of medical negligence. The wording of *Hunter* v *Hanley* is very clear. The view stated in a 1995 textbook dealing with the position in England that 'A good rule of thumb . . . is that if 10% of properly qualified practitioners in a given field would accept what was done as reasonable, then it was not negligent'[29] does not reflect the position in Scotland. If it is possible to find just one doctor (or dentist) whose opinion the court accept and who affirms that he or she would have followed the same course as the defender, then no matter how many contrary voices are heard, the pursuer will lose. The full effect of Lord President Clyde's words on an action raised in a Scottish court cannot be underestimated.

In *Coyle* v *Lothian Health Board*[30] a claim by the children of a man who died after a doctor failed to diagnose a myocardial infarction was unsuccessful. It was possible to show that there were warning signs in a scan seen by the doctor, but the court accepted that some doctors would have missed it. The extent of the variation from the norm on the trace was slight.

The judge also held that it was a matter of judgment by the doctor as to whether a patient should be admitted to hospital. A doctor was entitled to use her judgment and to make an assessment based on that professional opinion.

Legal basis for claims

Most actions by dissatisfied patients are based on allegations of negligence, arising from what the doctor or dentist did or what he failed to do. Whether it is a case of embarking on an unnecessary procedure, prescribing the wrong drugs, omitting to carry out appropriate tests or failing to recognise obvious symptoms, the same principles apply. The initial onus of proof is on the pursuer, and the standard of proof is the same as applies in any civil action, namely that of a balance of probabilities. Any suggestion that, because of the

[29] *Medical Negligence Litigation—A Practitioner's Guide*, p 8.
[30] 1991 SLT 277.

special tests contained in *Hunter* v *Hanley*, a writ alleging medical negligence imposes on the claimant a requirement to attain a higher standard has been firmly rejected by the Scottish courts.

Breach of contract

If the facts justify it, there is no reason why a doctor or dentist cannot be sued on the basis of an alleged breach of contract. If it can be proved that the practitioner failed to fulfil his part of the bargain, a valid claim might arise. A dentist who undertook to fill a gap successfully or to restore a damaged bridge to its former condition might be liable if he failed. Similarly, a cosmetic surgeon who promised 'wrinkle-free' results could be the subject of a successful action, if it could be shown that the undertaking was given and that the result did not conform to the promise. As with any suggested breach of contract, one of the major hurdles facing a pursuer is the need to prove the initial undertaking or promise.

Hsuing v *Webster*[31] was a claim which failed *inter alia* because the pursuer could not prove an undertaking that scarring would be covered by pubic hair and that after the operation her breasts would be symmetrical. The judge found that the results of the operations could have been due to poor marking or inappropriate tension but that this did not amount to negligence.

In *Dickson* v *The Hygienic Institute*[32] and *Lanphier* v *Phipos*[33] breach of contract was alleged. The latter, however, arose at a time when married women could not sue in their own right and is accordingly of less significance today.

Difficulties in achieving the necessary proof of a contractual relationship may have limited the number of 'contract-based' cases which reach court. Unless some form of written guarantee is obtained before the work, operation, treatment or procedure is started, it may be very difficult to prove that it is not just a case of somebody having his or her unreasonable hopes dashed by reality. In the absence of any document or independent proof, it may be necessary to rely on the defenders own notes, and they are unlikely to contain any explicit guarantee of total success.

Breach of contract can arise if the doctor is a superior or an employer of a nurse, receptionist or assistant. This can be the case in some private medical homes, where the owner may also be the resident doctor. It may also apply to dental practitioners so far as a hygienist or dental nurse is concerned, and it can arise if the receptionist of a GP practice is negligent in failing to relay an urgent call for help. The nature and conditions of employment, and what, if any, supervision is expected or required, can be important factors.

[31] 1992 SLT 1071.
[32] 1910 SC 352.
[33] (1838) 8 C & P 475.

In *Craig* v *McKendrick*[34] Lord Blades allowed an action against a doctor to proceed on the basis that, as the owner of a maternity nursing home, he was responsible for an alleged negligent act by the matron. It was averred that a baby had been burnt while in the matron's arms and that on the principle of *respondeat superior* the doctor owner could be made liable. The validity of the decision today is probably slight, bearing in mind that the claim arose at a time before the creation of the NHS.

The position of a surgeon working in the NHS was discussed in the case of *Fox* v *Glasgow & South-Western Hospitals Board*,[35] where it was alleged that Mr Fox had died owing to the negligence of a nurse. An attempt by the hospital board of management to involve the surgeon who had conducted an operation failed when the sole basis for seeking his inclusion was a suggestion that, as he was 'in charge' of the theatre, the nurses were acting under his control. Lord Strachan held that the board were liable as employers for any negligent act by a nurse in such circumstances. He rejected the contention that liability passed to the surgeon merely because he was the senior member of staff present. Unless it could be shown that the alleged negligent act resulted from instructions given by the surgeon (in which case responsibility would be personal and not based on any vicarious liability), the true employer remained at risk.

The action raised by Mrs Fox after the death of her husband on 21st April 1953 shows how quickly the wheels of justice could operate in those days. Not only was her case in progress 19 months later, it had proceeded to the point where, after the pleadings had been fully adjusted, a debate took place and the judge could send the case for trial by jury. The whole matter was resolved by 12th April 1955— less than two years after the sad event which had precipitated it. Nowadays it seems unlikely that such a speedy resolution would be attempted, which is perhaps unfortunate. (It is interesting to note that if the preliminary plea by the board had been successful there would have been sufficient time to raise another action before the triennium expired—a luxury which few are able to enjoy today.)

Where a junior doctor acts on faulty or inadequate instructions from a more senior colleague, he is not necessarily negligent. *Junor* v *McNicol*[36] made it clear, however, that a 'Nuremberg Defence' is not open to a qualified practitioner. Where the instructions provided by a senior doctor are obviously incorrect, a more junior practitioner cannot follow the suggested line and then avoid responsibility for his actions. As each health board has, since 1990, been responsible for the actings of all its employees, the point is probably academic. The board would be obliged to pay, whether the fault lay with the

[34] 1948 SLT (Notes) 91.
[35] 1955 SLT 337.
[36] [1959] CLY 2255.

consultant (for the poor instructions) or with the junior doctor (for acting as he did).

Acting within the scope of competence and experience

There is a responsibility on a doctor to act within the scope of his or her competence and experience. In *Steward* v *Greater Glasgow Health Board*[37] Lord Keith stated that a practitioner should seek help if required and that a failure to do so, if circumstances and time permitted, could, if an avoidable injury occurred, amount to negligence. The case arose out of a claim by the parents of a baby allegedly brain damaged in the course of a complicated delivery. The judge held that negligence had not been shown, deciding that the doctors concerned had acted in accordance with acceptable medical practice in the emergency situation with which they were faced.

In *Jones* v *Manchester Corporation*[38] it was held that a hospital board which allowed a doctor with inadequate experience to administer Pentothal were liable for any resulting disaster by permitting her to act outwith her knowledge and experience. Dr Wilkes had been qualified for only five months when she injected the barbiturate in a dosage which would have been acceptable for a conscious patient but was fatal for a man who was already under an anaesthetic. Although Manchester Regional Hospital Board were liable as employers for Dr Wilkes's error, a great deal of the argument revolved round whether their liability was vicarious or whether, 'by getting inexperienced doctors to perform their duties for them, without adequate supervision',[39] they were themselves negligent. Denning LJ (as he then was) held that they were.

A doctor must act within the scope of his experience and knowledge; he must also be fit enough to carry out his duties competently. An attempt was made in *Nickolls* v *Ministry of Health*[40] to show that, because a surgeon was known to have lung cancer, he was unfit to perform a goitre operation which resulted in permanent damage to the patient's throat. The court held on the facts, first, that there was no evidence of negligence and, secondly, that despite his own serious condition, the surgeon was fit enough to perform the operation.

[37] 1976 SLT (Notes) 66 (quantum only).
[38] [1952] 2 All ER 125; [1952] 2 QB 852.
[39] [1952] 2 All ER 125 at p 133.
[40] [1955] CLY 1902.

Chapter 4

DUTY OF CARE AND THE IMPORTANCE OF CONSENT

The duty of care which the law places on all doctors and dentists is different from that which applies to others. Unlike the situation which normally applies, an error of judgment by a doctor or dentist does not necessarily result in a finding of negligence. Lord Fraser of Tullybelton summarised the position in his judgment in *Whitehouse* v *Jordan*:[1]

> 'The true position is that an error of judgment may, or may not, be negligent; it depends on the nature of the error. If it is one that would not have been made by a reasonably competent professional man professing to have the standard and type of skill that the defender held himself out as having, and acting with ordinary care, then it is negligent. If, on the other hand, it is an error that such a man, acting with ordinary care, might have made, then it is not negligent.'

The contrast between that standard and the one which is applicable in a normal case involving an allegation of negligence is obvious. In Scotland, and probably in England following its adoption in *Maynard* v *West Midlands Regional Health Authority*,[2] the tests for an action concerning medical negligence are again to be found in *Hunter* v *Hanley*.[3] In his reasons for ordering a fresh jury trial, Lord President Clyde summarised the position in a passage which has remained largely unchallenged since its pronouncement in 1955:[4]

> 'To succeed in an action based on negligence, whether against a doctor or anyone else, it is of course necessary to establish a breach of that duty to take care which the law requires, and the degree of want of care which constitutes negligence must vary with the circumstances.'

[1] [1981] 1 All ER 267 (HL) at p 281.
[2] [1985] 1 All ER 635.
[3] 1955 SC 200; 1955 SLT 213.
[4] 1955 SC 200 at p 204.

That statement of the law followed the opinion of Lord Wright in *Caswell* v *Powell Duffryn Associated Collieries*.[5] The Lord President then applied the principles behind *Caswell* to the specific issue in *Hunter* v *Hanley* namely, what standards does the law seek to impose on medical practitioners, and against what are these standards to be measured. He continued:[6]

> 'But where the conduct of a doctor, or indeed any professional man, is concerned, the circumstances are not so precise and clear cut as in a normal case. In the realm of diagnosis and treatment there is ample scope for genuine difference of opinion and one man is not negligent merely because his conclusion differs from that of other professional men, nor because he has displayed less skill or knowledge than others would have shown. The true test for establishing negligence in diagnosis or treatment on the part of a doctor is whether he has been proved to be guilty of such failure that no doctor of ordinary skill would be guilty of if acting with ordinary care.'

Later cases established that the views delivered in *Hunter* v *Hanley* apply equally to dentists; had *Hunter* v *Hanley* concerned an injection by a dental practitioner instead of, as it did, a doctor, there is no doubt that Lord Clyde and his fellow judges would have expressed themselves in identical terms.

In *Todd* v *Butler*[7] the principles of *Hunter* v *Hanley* were applied to the duty of care owed by a dentist. A patient complained that she had suffered a cut under her tongue when an airotor drill had slipped. It was held that allowing the drill to slip amounted to negligence in terms of *Hunter*. The dentist gave the court an explanation as to how the injury had occurred (by the patient moving her tongue suddenly), but this was rejected by the sheriff.

In *Aird* v *Ramsay*[8] the pursuer was unsuccessful in her claim after a reamer fractured during treatment of an incisor tooth. Sheriff Presslie noted that 'the appropriate authority for the court to consider was contained in *Hunter* v *Hanley*'.

Consent

Most medical, and practically all surgical and dental, treatment involves a degree of physical contact. What would, under other circumstances, amount to an assault is covered by the implied or actual consent of the patient. The consent, once given, can be withdrawn at any time and does not entitle a doctor or dentist to stray outwith its implied terms.

[5] [1940] AC 152.
[6] 1955 SC 200 at p 206.
[7] 1996 GWD 9-514.
[8] Glasgow Sheriff Court, unreported, 5th December 1984.

In the criminal case of *Hussain* v *Houston*[9] a doctor was convicted of assault after it was held that he had exceeded the bounds of any implied consent. In *Hussain*, a consultant in accident and emergency argued that a patient who attends at a hospital, and invites a qualified doctor to carry out an examination in connection with her injuries or symptoms, is consenting to a full medical examination, and that the consent remains in effect unless and until it is specifically withdrawn. Dr Hussain therefore argued that once the patient had by asking him to deal with her injuries, given her consent to a medical examination, he could not be guilty of a crime, or at least that he could not be committing an assault. The appeal court refused to quash either the conviction or the three-month prison sentence which followed. The court affirmed that any examination had to be a proper medical one, and that a doctor is not given a *carte blanche* by any implied consent. They agreed with the lower court's view which rejected the argument that

> 'a doctor, once he is allowed to carry out a medical examination, is entitled to do as he wishes, even if he ventures into parts of the body which have nothing whatever to do with the complaint made, and that he has an implied consent to continue to touch, probe and fondle any part of the body unless and until the patient indicates that she wishes it to stop'.

Even if a criminal charge does not follow, a doctor or dentist can be liable in damages if the limits of a consent are exceeded. An instance of this occurred when a surgeon, while carrying out an operation for which he had a valid and full consent, noticed what to him was an unsightly mole on the patient's thigh. Having completed the original operation, and while the patient was still under a general anaesthetic, he removed the growth. The patient, who claimed that he had been emotionally as well as physically attached to the blemish, was successful in his quest for compensation for his loss.

A decision in England in 1995 illustrates the extent to which a court will go to restrict a doctor's authority to proceed beyond the limits of an expressed consent. In *Bartley* v *Studd*[10] the patient had given her written consent for a hysterectomy. In the course of the operation the surgeon decided also to remove the ovaries—a procedure for which he had no consent and for which there was no immediate medical justification. Mrs Bartley was successful in a claim based on an allegation of negligence and she also persuaded the court to rule that the doctor's action amounted to battery or an assault. In both cases it is apparent that had the patient been asked to give his or her agreement to the proposed course of action, it would have been withheld.

[9] 1995 SLT 1060.
[10] Unreported, 6th July 1995.

Where a patient is not concerned as to the procedure, the position may be different. Such a situation occurred in *Thomson* v *Devon*[11] when a convict in custody was vaccinated by a doctor. In the court's judgment refusing a crave for compensation for assault, it was noted that the pursuer did not care one way or the other. Although he knew and understood what was happening, his position was that 'he neither consented nor objected to the operation'. That may have been the approach taken by the court at the turn of the century, but it is unlikely that a judge nowadays would be allowed to ignore the rights of a prisoner, who by the very nature of his confinement is more vulnerable than others. The European Court of Human Rights would undoubtedly regard forced inoculation as an assault justifying, at least, a civil claim for damages.

The main point in *Thomson* v *Devon*, however, is that in normal cases specific consent is not always required. A patient, by attending a doctor or dentist with an obvious injury or complaint, is presumably agreeing to the practitioner doing what is necessary to effect a cure. Problems can arise, however, where treatment involves a risk or where there are various options to be considered. In such circumstances the patient might choose not to proceed with the suggested treatment or to seek another opinion before reaching a final decision.

Obtaining consent

There is no set method of obtaining or recording consent. It can be oral, implied or in writing. Occasions can arise where a patient may be too ill to agree formally to a course of treatment. If a doctor is faced with such a situation, he will use his clinical judgment and proceed if appropriate. Nobody would expect a doctor to delay giving essential care merely because it has proved impossible to get a consent at the time.

Because it is necessary in normal circumstances to have a consent before embarking upon an invasive procedure, it is usual, where possible, to get it in writing so that there is a permanent record of the patient agreeing to what otherwise would be an assault. It is, however, not essential that the patient signs a form. Provided the agreement is recorded in the medical notes, there is a contemporaneous history to which reference can be made.

Experience has shown that if asked about it later, many patients do not recall having signified their agreement. This is especially so if a problem has subsequently arisen. An adviser should check the whole of the hospital records before accusing a doctor of exceeding his authority. Practitioners nowadays usually ensure that a nurse or another doctor is present when consent is sought and obtained. That

[11] (1899) 15 Sh Ct Rep 209.

witness's presence will probably be recorded in the relevant medical records; it may also be mentioned in the nursing Kardex.

Child's consent

The difficulties which can arise over the ability of a child to give a legally acceptable consent are dealt with in the Age of Legal Capacity (Scotland) Act 1991. Section 2(4) provides:

> 'A person under the age of 16 years shall have the legal capacity to consent on his own behalf to any surgical, medical or dental procedure or treatment where, in the opinion of a qualified medical practitioner attending him, he is capable of understanding the nature and possible consequences of the procedure or treatment.'

A child of any age can therefore give a valid consent. The three important factors which are prerequisites for such a consent are:

1 that it is a 'qualified medical practitioner' who requires to be satisfied about the child's ability to comprehend and assess any information;

2 that the qualified medical practitioner is 'attending' the patient (thereby ruling out any hospital official, however highly qualified unless he is directly involved in the child's medical care or management); and

3 that the doctor is satisfied as to the child's 'understanding [of] the nature and the possible consequences of the procedure or treatment'.

Although the section does not mention dentists specifically, the reference to 'dental procedure or treatment' makes it clear that a qualified dental practitioner is in the same position as his medical colleague. The Act, however, does not give any right to a nurse, receptionist or hygienist to substitute for the doctor or dentist.

Most practitioners will record the fact that consent has been sought and obtained, and in the case of a child the notes ought to show the name of the qualified practitioner involved. In making an assessment as to whether the child 'is capable of understanding the nature and possible consequences of the procedure or treatment', a doctor or dentist will require to consider the age of the patient, his intelligence and the nature and complexities of any procedure, as well as what risks there are.

There are no set rules as to when a child should or should not be involved in the consent process, and it is extremely unlikely that a court would accept a challenge to a doctor's professional judgment as to whether a child could give a valid consent.

Because Parliament recognised that young people should have the right to challenge prejudicial agreements they had entered into, s 3 of the Age of Legal Capacity (Scotland) Act 1991 gives anybody under the age of 21 the right to have an agreement entered into between the ages of 16 and 18 set aside if it is a 'prejudicial transaction'. Section 3(3), however, excludes from this provision 'any surgical, medical or dental procedure or treatment'.

Accordingly, somebody aged 16 or 17 who has given his consent to a medical or dental operation, cannot look to the terms of s 3 for a foundation on which to base a challenge to it. In this regard his situation is similar to that of an adult who agrees to something and later, in the light of developments—and with that most valuable of all tools, a chance to see things in retrospect—regrets the decision.

Although in terms of the Act a child, provided he understands the factors involved, can give a valid consent, it is usually a parent or legal guardian who is approached by the doctor. When the child is too young to comprehend adequately, then in common law and in terms of the Children (Scotland) Act 1995 a parent can give consent to any medical procedure, on the basis that it is for the welfare of the child. Where a parent refuses to agree to what is, in the opinion of qualified medical practitioners, proper and necessary treatment, the matter can be referred to a children's hearing.

In the case of *Finlayson, Applicant*[12] Sheriff Scott held that parents who had been fully advised of the consequences of refusing or delaying orthodox treatment for their haemophiliac son were showing a lack of parental care by refusing to agree to treatment, including blood transfusions. The sheriff concluded that there were sufficient grounds to justify a referral of the child to a hearing as possibly being in need of care, in terms of s 32(1), (2) of the Social Work (Scotland) Act 1968, as amended. That part of the legislation provided that

'(1) A child may be in need of compulsory measures of care . . . if any of the conditions mentioned in the next following subsection is satisfied with respect to him.

(2) The conditions referred to in subsection (1) of this section are that— . . .

(c) lack of parental care is likely to cause him unnecessary suffering or seriously to impair his health and development'.

The section has been replaced by s 52 of the Children (Scotland) Act 1995. Although the sheriff was clear that both parents loved their son and had what they considered to be sound reasons for their stand, he was satisfied that the medical evidence was such that there was a risk to the health and possibly the life of the child. This meant that there was an apparent need for compulsory care as envisaged in the legislation.

A not dissimilar situation arose in England in *Re B (A Minor)*,[13] when the parents of a Down's syndrome child refused to give their consent

[12] (Sh Ct) 1989 SCLR 601.
[13] [1981] 1 WLR 1421.

to an operation which was essential to clear an intestinal blockage. Because of their daughter's condition and the possibility that she would die anyway within a few months, they were of the view that it would be kinder to allow her to die rather than subject her to the operation.

The local authority intervened and having made the girl a ward of court claimed that they had the power to authorise the surgeon to proceed. He refused to do so, arguing that the wishes of the parents should not be overruled, but the Court of Appeal supported the local authority and instructed a different consultant to carry out the operation.

Section 5(1) of the Children (Scotland) Act 1995 deals with the situation which arises when consent is sought from somebody, who although aged at least 16 and having 'care and control' of a child, does not have parental responsibilities or parental rights, as defined in ss 1(3) and 2(4). Such a person can give the necessary consent where:

'(a) the child is not able to give such consent on his own behalf; and

(b) it is not within the knowledge of the person that a parent of the child would refuse to give the consent in question.'

Section 58(5) authorises a sheriff, when granting a child protection order, to include a direction allowing

'(a) any examination as to the physical or mental state of the child;

(b) any other assessment or interview of the child; or

(c) any treatment of the child arising out of such an examination or assessment'.

This section is not included in the list of circumstances where the child retains a right to refuse an examination or treatment. Otherwise, where a child has the necessary capacity in terms of s 2(4) of the Age of Legal Capacity (Scotland) Act 1991, then while the child is the subject of a warrant or a supervision requirement from a children's hearing, no examination or treatment can take place unless the child consents (s 90 of the 1995 Act).

Consent and the incapax
The position of an adult who is incapable of giving consent was considered by Lord McLean in *L, Petitioner*.[14] He stated that the correct test to be applied in a case where authority for a ward's surgical sterilisation was sought was whether it was 'in the best interests of

[14] (OH) 1996 SCLR 538 (Notes).

41

the ward'. That approach was expressly approved by Lord President Hope and Lord Cullen in their judgments in the five-bench decision in *Law Hospital NHS Trust* v *Lord Advocate*.[15]

Commenting on the view expressed in *L*, Lord Hope, after noting that Lord McLean had considered that the best interests of the patient was the correct test to apply, stated:[16]

> 'In my opinion we should approve of the application of that test in such cases, where the issue is whether a tutor-dative should be authorised to consent to medical treatment of the ward. And I believe that we should also hold that it is the test which must be applied by the court when deciding whether or not to authorise the withholding of treatment in cases . . . where treatment is necessary if life is to continue.'

Lord Milligan expressed some concern at such a wide-reaching proposal. Although agreeing that the correct test was 'the best interests of the ward', he added:[17]

> 'I have considerable difficulty with the application of such a test in the circumstances of a proposed withdrawal of treatment case. . . . Parliament will no doubt require to grapple in due course with the thorny problems of the implication of altruistic sentiments and the relevance, if any at all, of interests other than those of the patient.'

It seems reasonably clear that each case involving the deliberate withdrawal of treatment will require to be considered individually and decided upon its own facts and circumstances. The Lord Advocate has indicated that practitioners who follow the terms of any authorisation given in a particular case will not be liable for prosecution.

Informed consent
Experience shows that the likelihood of there being a written form of consent increases with the complexity of the treatment and any possible side effects, but there is no compulsion on a doctor or dentist to obtain an agreement in writing. However, in the absence of any such record, it is more difficult for the practitioner to satisfy a court, perhaps many years later, that the patient agreed to the course of treatment undertaken and was advised of any known risks. This is particularly so if the final result turns out to be below the pursuer's hopes and expectations. In that event it is a natural reaction to believe that the possible problems were not explained at the time, or that formal consent was never sought. Again, an adviser should check any records before assuming that the client's recall is perfect.

---

[15] (IH) 1996 SCLR 491; (OH) 1996 SCLR 566 (Updates); 1996 SLT 848.
[16] 1996 SCLR 491 at p 505.
[17] Ibid, p 517.

Forty or fifty years ago it was unlikely that a patient would expect or be offered much information before being asked for his consent. The belief that 'the doctor knows best' prevailed and most people were quite content to remain in ignorance as to what a particular operation entailed, what the after effects would be, and what risks attached to the procedure. Nowadays the situation is different and there has been a rapid development of 'openness'.

Disclosure of risks
One of the findings made by Lord Caplan in *Moyes* v *Lothian Health Board*[18] was that there had been a dramatic alteration in medical opinion as to whether a patient needed to be informed of a particular risk factor, and if so, how much detail should be provided. In the time between the operation which gave rise to the claim and the hearing in the Court of Session (a period of less than seven years), there had been a complete reversal in the ratio of those doctors who felt the need to inform their patients of a recognised, if slight, risk of an adverse side effect and those who chose not to burden their patients with such knowledge.

Among the various points which *Moyes* v *Lothian Health Board* reaffirmed was that the date at which the state of knowledge of doctors is to be judged, or inquiry made as to their practice in relation to the providing of information to a patient, is the date of the incident and not that of the proof. In affirming this, Lord Caplan was following a long line of authorities both in Scotland and England, all of which have expressed the same view in different words. None has put it in clearer terms than Lord Denning, when in the Appeal Court hearing in *Roe* v *Minister of Health*[19] he commented: 'We must not look at the 1947 incident with 1954 spectacles.'

The mere giving of a consent is only part of the picture. Without the patient's agreement, most medical or dental procedures would probably constitute an assault. Although it could be usually argued that there is an element of implied consent in that the person attended at the surgery or hospital and presumably intended that action should be taken to deal with his problem, it is a totally different matter as to whether an adequately informed consent has been sought. The medical profession, and to a lesser extent the dental profession, has wrestled for a number of years with the dilemma as to how much, and under what circumstances, a patient should be made aware of a known risk factor, how much detail needs to be given and whether it should be left to the patient to ask questions. One of the concerns is that some nervous people, learning of an infinitesimal chance of disaster, will refuse essential and possibly life-saving treatment. Others may, through undue anxiety, worsen their condition.

[18] 1990 SLT 444.
[19] [1954] 2 QB 66.

For more than 200 hundred years it has been clear that a doctor cannot proceed without having the consent, implied or otherwise, of the patient. In *Slater* v *Baker and Stapleton*,[20] where a surgeon wanted to try an experiment with a new instrument and failed to tell his patient or seek his agreement before using it to rebreak a limb, it was held that 'it is reasonable that a patient should be told what is about to be done to him, that he may take courage and put himself in such a situation as to enable him to undergo the operation'. The final words reflect the absence of an effective anaesthetic in 1767!

The mid-1980s saw a number of cases in England which explored the question as to who could give or withhold consent, and how detailed any information needed to be. The decision in *Gillick* v *West Norfolk and Wisbech Area Health Authority*[21] has now, so far as Scotland is concerned, been superseded by the Age of Legal Capacity (Scotland) Act 1991. The action concerned a mother's attempt to prevent doctors giving contraceptive advice to her daughters who were then aged under 16. The use of the term 'procedure or treatment' in s 2(4) of the 1991 Act, where it refers to 'any . . . medical . . . procedure or treatment' covers the giving of advice as well as, if necessary, the supply of contraceptives.

While the case of *Gillick* v *West Norfolk and Wisbech Area Health Authority* was being considered by the Court of Appeal, and before the House of Lords had had a chance to give the definitive view on its peculiar facts, another case reached that august body, enabling their Lordships to review the whole question of consent and how far it was necessary to advise and counsel a patient.

When the five Lords of Appeal considered the English case of *Sidaway* v *Board of Governors of the Bethlem Royal Hospital and the Maudsley Hospital*[22] they were referred to a vast range of decisions made in other countries and jurisdictions. These included the judgment in *Chatterton* v *Gerson*[23] where the patient had been unsuccessful in a claim based on allegations that the physician had failed to explain the procedure adequately and that accordingly she had been the victim of an assault or an act of negligence. Bristow J stated that each court must look at the particular facts and then ask, 'Was there a real consent?' He went on to express a view as to how far it was necessary for a claimant to go to prove that the purported agreement was void:[24]

> 'I think justice requires that in order to vitiate the reality of consent there must be a greater failure of communication between doctor and patient than that involved in a breach of duty if the claim is based on negligence. When the claim is based

---

[20] (1767) 2 Wils 359.
[21] [1985] 3 All ER 402.
[22] [1985] 1 All ER 643.
[23] [1981] 1 All ER 257.
[24] Ibid, p 265.

on negligence the plaintiff must prove not only the breach of duty to inform but that had the duty not been broken she would not have chosen to have the operation. Where the claim is based on trespass to the person, once it is shown that the consent is unreal, then what the plaintiff would have decided if she had been given the information which would have prevented vitiation of the reality of her consent is irrelevant.

'In my judgment once the patient is informed in broad terms of the nature of the procedure which is intended, and gives consent, that consent is real, and the cause of the action on which to base a claim for failure to go into the risks and implications is negligence, not trespass.'

He thereafter ruled on what a doctor is required to do if an allegation of negligence is to be avoided. Referring to the views expressed by McNair J in *Bolam v Friern Hospital Management Committee*[25] and by Lord Denning in *Hatcher v Black*,[26] he concluded:[27]

'The duty of the doctor is to explain what he intends to do, and its implications, in the way a careful and responsible doctor in similar circumstances would have done.'

The judge considered how far a doctor has to go in informing a patient. He concluded that

'there is no obligation on the doctor to canvass with the patient anything other than the inherent implications of the particular operation he intends to carry out . . . he ought to warn of what may happen by misfortune however well the operation is done. . . . In what he says any good doctor has to take into account the personality of the patient, the likelihood of the misfortune, and what in the way of warning is for the particular patient's welfare.'[28]

The arguments advanced in the House of Lords in *Sidaway v Board of Governors of the Bethlem Royal Hospital and the Maudsley Hospital* illustrated the wide scope of approaches adopted elsewhere and reinforced the need for a definitive statement of the law in England from the highest judicial forum. In Canada the decisions in *Reibl v Hughes*[29] (to which reference was made in *Chatterton v Gerson*) and *Videto v Kennedy*[30] showed that although each case had to be looked at in the light of the particular circumstances, and in particular the possible effect of disclosure on the welfare of the patient, the trend towards openness was to be encouraged.

[25] [1957] 1 WLR 582.
[26] [1954] CLY 2289.
[27] [1981] 1 All ER 257 at p 265.
[28] Ibid, p 266.
[29] (1980) 114 DLR (3d) 1 (SCC); (1980) CLY 2613.
[30] [1980] CLY 1894.

The decision in *Sidaway* v *Board of Governors of the Bethlem Royal Hospital and the Maudsley Hospital* was by a majority. In a strongly worded dissenting opinion Lord Scarman supported the approach of 'openness' which prevails in parts of the USA following the 1972 decision of *Canterbury* v *Spence*.[31] He would, however have refused the appeal even if the law had been as he wished, concluding that the plaintiff's claim failed no matter which approach one took. The views expressed in *Chatterton* v *Gerson* received approval.

Mrs Sidaway, who was aged 64, had suffered from persistent pain in her neck and shoulders for many years. She sought medical advice and for 14 years she was seen by a consultant neuro-surgeon, Mr Murray Falconer. The doctor finally recommended that she undergo an operation to her spinal column with a view to relieving the pain. Mr Falconer warned Mrs Sidaway of the possibility of disturbing a nerve root as well as what consequences might flow from such a misfortune. It was contended on the patient's behalf that he should have advised her of the risk of spinal cord damage, but failed to do so. During the 1974 operation, to which Mrs Sidaway had given her consent on the basis of the information given to her, she was rendered severely disabled as the result of damage to her spinal column.

She sued the hospital authority as the surgeon's employers as well as Mr Falconer himself. Unfortunately, by the time the matter came to proof, Mr Falconer had died and this, in the words of Lord Scarman, 'presents difficulties' for the claimant. What the effect on Mrs Sidaway's claim would have been if a trial judge had been able to assess the consultant's reasons for what advice he gave, and what he withheld, is a matter for speculation. What is clear from all the judgments in the House of Lords is that a court will not lessen the burden on a claimant if a delay in bringing proceedings has, by death or other factors, diminished the possible sources of primary evidence.

Those advising patients who consider that they may have a claim would do well to consider the additional burdens which Mrs Sidaway's legal team faced when nearly eight years after the fateful operation they managed to get the case to proof.

The judge at the original hearing concluded that Mr Falconer's diagnosis had been correct, that his recommendation of operative treatment had been reasonable and proper, and that he performed the operation with skill and care. None of these findings was challenged on appeal. Accordingly, the sole important question which required to be addressed was whether Mrs Sidaway should have been advised about the risk (estimated at less than 1 per cent) that Mr Falconer could damage her spinal cord in the course of the operation. She

[31] (1972) 464 F 2d 772.

argued that had she been fully informed, she could have decided not to proceed with the operation; by not giving her the essential information she claimed that she was deprived of her right to make an informed choice.

Mr Justice Skinner rejected this heading of claim and Mrs Sidaway was no more successful before the Court of Appeal. Her final hope lay with the House of Lords and there Lords Scarman, Diplock, Keith, Bridge and Templeman heard three days of argument which included consideration of *Hunter v Hanley, Bolam v Friern Hospital Management Committee* and the then unreported case of *Maynard v West Midlands Regional Health Authority*. In the judgments delivered in February 1985, a clear divergence of views can be seen. All five were in favour of refusing the appeal but their reasons differed.

Lord Diplock, whose opinion found support from the line adopted by Lords Keith and Bridge, summarised his view when he concluded his judgment:[32]

> 'To decide what risks the existence of which a patient should be voluntarily warned and the terms in which such a warning, if any, should be given, having regard to the effect that the warning may have, is as much an exercise of professional skill and judgment as any other part of the doctor's comprehensive duty of care to the individual patient, and expert medical evidence on this matter should be treated in just the same way. The *Bolam* test should be applied.'

Lord Bridge, in a passage which can be used in any action relating to medical negligence, stated:[33]

> 'Broadly, a doctor's professional functions may be divided into three phases: diagnosis, advice and treatment. In performing his functions of diagnosis and treatment, the standard by which English law measures the doctor's duty of care to his patient is not open to doubt.'

He reaffirmed that *Bolam v Friern Hospital Management Committee* and *Hunter v Hanley* were the basis of the 'firmly established law' on such matters. He then considered whether the same principles applied to the third element, namely advice, before, having reviewed the two possible extremes, he concluded that it did. In his view:[34]

> '[A] decision [of] what degree of disclosure of risks is best calculated to assist a patient to make a rational choice whether or not to undergo a particular treatment must primarily be a matter of clinical judgment. It would follow from this that the issue whether non-disclosure in a particular case should be condemned as a breach of a doctor's duty of care is an issue to be

[32] [1985] 1 All ER 643 at p 659.
[33] Ibid, p 660.
[34] Ibid, pp 662–663.

decided primarily on the basis of medical evidence, applying the *Bolam* test.'

Lord Scarman, in his dissenting opinion, said that he found a complete approach to this aspect of medical care based solely on the *Bolam* v *Friern Hospital Management Committee* principles 'disturbing'. He favoured following the line taken in the District of Columbia Appeal Court in *Crain* v *Allison*,[35] when they affirmed the earlier decision of *Canterbury* v *Spence*. The doctrine was only accepted in certain states of the USA, but had found approval in the Supreme Court of Canada in *Reibl* v *Hughes*. Explaining the basis for, and the consequences flowing from, *Canterbury*, Lord Scarman said:[36]

'In *Canterbury* v *Spence* the court enunciated certain propositions. (1) The root premise is the concept that every human being of adult years and of sound mind has a right to determine what shall be done with his own body. (2) The consent is the informed exercise of a choice, and that entails an opportunity to evaluate knowledgeably the options available and the risks attendant on each. (3) The doctor must, therefore, disclose all "material risks"; what risks are "material" is determined by the "prudent patient" test, which was formulated by the court:
    "(a) risk is . . . material when a reasonable person, in what the physician knows or should know to be the patient's position, would be likely to attach significance to the risk or cluster of risks in deciding whether or not to forego the proposed therapy".'

The remaining Lords of Appeal rejected that viewpoint, and in England the position remains that the decisions in *Bolam* v *Friern Hospital Management Committee* and *Maynard* v *West Midlands Regional Health Authority* set out the guiding principles in all cases of medical negligence whether it relates to treatment, diagnosis or advice.

The decision in *Sidaway* v *Board of Governors of the Bethlem Royal Hospital and the Maudsley Hospital*, together with the detailed reasons for the majority view, was studied carefully in Scotland, as elsewhere. The dissenting judgment, because it was in clear terms, was pronounced by a Law Lord whose opinions carried considerable weight and because it reflected a body of opinion favouring a complete openness in such matters, was studied equally carefully. The chance for a Scottish court to consider *Sidaway* and in particular to see whether it had weakened the authority of *Hunter* v *Hanley* was awaited with interest.

The opportunity to ascertain whether the Court of Session would (1) follow *Sidaway* v *Board of Governors of the Bethlem Royal Hospital and the Maudsley Hospital*, (2) adopt the American attitude expressed in

---

[35] (1982) 443 A 2d 558.
[36] [1985] 1 All ER 643 at p 653.

Canterbury v *Spence* (as approved by Lord Scarman in his dissenting judgment) or (3) set its own line in the delicate field of 'informed consent' came in the case *Moyes* v *Lothian Health Board*.[37]

The background to Mrs Moyes's action was complex and although Lord Caplan finally based his decision on the reliability of the witnesses, he dealt with the arguments in relation to how much (if at all) it is necessary for a doctor to provide a patient with an analysis of possible risk factors. In doing so he considered the individual judgments given in the House of Lords in *Sidaway* v *Board of Governors of the Bethlem Royal Hospital and the Maudsley Hospital* and commented on various passages in the opinions of Lords Bridge, Keith and Templeman.

Mrs Moyes had suffered from migraine pain for a number of years prior to 1980. At that time, when she was aged 40, she developed a severe pain on the left side of her face which extended from the centre of the cheek towards her head. The new pain was different from the migraine attacks both in location and intensity. Neither her GP nor the Ear Nose and Throat Department of the Edinburgh Royal Infirmary could discover the cause. Finally Mrs Moyes was seen by the Professor of Surgical Neurology in the same hospital, Professor J. D. Miller.

To assist in his search for a possible cause, Professor Miller arranged for the patient to undergo a computed tomography (CT) scan, which was undertaken by a consultant neuro-radiologist. The procedure involved injecting Mrs Moyes with a contrast medium to enhance the images recorded by the scan. The report on the scanning indicated that it was normal, thereby eliminating a tumour as a possible reason for the patient's continued facial pain. There was no indication in the report that Mrs Moyes had complained of any adverse side effect from the procedure.

The Professor considered that the scan might have failed to reveal a vascular problem. He therefore recommended that his patient should undergo an investigation using angiography. This involved a further injection of a contrast medium, this time into the cerebral blood vessels. The effect would be that once the vessels were opaque, a radiologist could inspect them using special X-ray equipment. The same consultant as had reviewed the CT scan was involved, and it was his practice to undertake angiography only when the patient was under a general anaesthetic.

In January 1982 Mrs Moyes attended at the hospital and, having seen Professor Miller, signed a consent form. The following day, while she was under an anaesthetic, the usual contrast medium (an iodine-based preparation) was injected into her. During the course of the investigation she suffered a blockage in her cerebral vascular system causing a stroke. Although the procedure was stopped immediately,

[37] 1990 SLT 444.

and every possible step was taken to rectify the situation, Mrs Moyes was left with a permanent weakness in her left arm as well as an impaired memory.

She sued the health board as the employers of the various doctors involved. She contended that there was a known risk of between 0.2 and 0.3 per cent of a patient having significant neurological problems (including a stroke) as the result of angiography. She maintained that the risk was greater in her case because of her previous history of migraines as well as an adverse reaction which, she claimed, had followed the initial procedure. She therefore contended that, because of the known risk, the later procedure should not have been undertaken, or at least the true dangers should have been explained to her before she gave her consent to the investigation. She alleged that had she been made aware of the risk and potential dangers involved in angiography, especially in her particular circumstances, she would not have given her consent.

Mrs Moyes failed to prove that there had been an adverse reaction to the CT scan and Lord Caplan accepted the evidence of the doctors that she was warned of the possible risks of complications, including a stroke, when her consent was being sought. The claim therefore failed on issues of credibility and reliability. The judge, however, took the opportunity to consider what obligations there are on a medical practitioner to advise a patient of a known risk factor, and whether detailed or merely general advice should be offered.

Counsel for Mrs Moyes argued that the views expressed in *Sidaway* v *Board of Governors of the Bethlem Royal Hospital and the Maudsley Hospital* changed the basis of the law away from the principles enshrined in *Hunter* v *Hanley* and *Bolam* v *Friern Hospital Management Committee*. Lord Caplan rejected that contention when he stated:[38]

'In my view the *Sidaway* case in no way alters the pre-existing view of the law that the appropriate tests to apply in medical negligence cases are to be found in *Hunter* v *Hanley* and *Bolam*.'

He continued:[39]

'As I see it the law in both Scotland and England has come down firmly against the view that the doctor's duty to the patient involves at all costs obtaining the informed consent of the patient to specific medical treatments. When the patient entrusts himself to the doctor he expects, and is entitled, to be kept fully informed about decisions which have to be taken and which may concern his welfare, but the paramount expectation is that the doctor will do what is best to care for the patient's health. In general it will be consistent with that primary responsibility that the doctor should acquaint the patient with the risks facing him and that

---

[38] Ibid, p 449.
[39] Ibid.

becomes particularly critical when the risk is a severe risk for as Lord Bridge observes in *Sidaway* in such a case the patient may want to be able to decide whether he should submit himself to a significant risk or even secure a second opinion. However, I can read nothing in the majority view in *Sidaway* which suggests that the extent and quality of warning to be given by a doctor to his patient should not in the last resort be governed by medical criteria.'

Lord Caplan then considered some of the situations in which medical criteria might prevail and continued:[40]

'The risks inherent in a particular operation or procedure, the manner in which the operation may affect or damage a particular patient, the medical need for the operation, and the ability of the patient to absorb information about his situation without adding damage to his health are all matters where the doctor, with his own clinical experience and the benefit of the experience of other practitioners, is best able to form a judgment as to what the patient can be safely told in the exercise of medical care. Nor is it practical or necessary that the patient should be told of every risk.'

The judge therefore concluded that

'it might be a matter of fine clinical judgment as to whether a patient should be alarmed by being told about a remote risk when this has to be balanced against the possibility of causing the patient unnecessary worry and distress which could render the treatment more difficult or might in some cases even discourage him from going through with an essential operation'.[41]

Referring again to Lord Bridge's opinion in *Sidaway v Board of Governors of the Bethlem Royal Hospital and the Maudsley Hospital*, Lord Caplan opined that

'in questions of medical practice where the skill or the knowledge, or specialist experience of the doctor is the material factor, standards will be regulated by the standards of responsible members of the profession'.[42]

He added that 'what falls within the ambit of medical expertise should not be regarded too closely', before summarising his view of what requires to be considered in such cases:[43]

'The ultimate test is whether the doctor has shown reasonable care for the safety of his patient so that if it can be shown that the doctor's conduct is manifestly lacking in respect of the discharge of that responsibility it will not avail to say that other doctors

[40] Ibid.
[41] Ibid.
[42] Ibid, p 450.
[43] Ibid.

follow the same practice. Recognition by the doctor of the adult patient's right to make decisions about the risks he incurs is essentially an aspect of the duty to take reasonable care for his safety.'

After the noting that Lord Templeman regarded a doctor's position on this matter as one based on contractual responsibility whereas Lords Bridge and Keith referred to a duty of care, Lord Caplan stated:[44]

'Whether or not a particular practice can be condemned on the basis of the general duty to show care (or contractual duty to disclose risks) as distinct from purely medical considerations will depend on the circumstances. However, a particular example of a practice which would be condemned on general considerations is the case where a patient is not warned of a decidedly substantial risk which might arise from an operation. In such a case the patient's safety is obviously imperilled and he has the right to make a decision as to whether he will accept the risk unless there are very clear medical reasons for denying him that election.'

One such reason could be if the patient was not *compos mentis*. It is, however, clear from the views expressed in *Sidaway v Board of Governors of the Bethlem Royal Hospital and the Maudsley Hospital* and *Moyes v Lothian Health Board* that it will normally be necessary for a court to look at the precise circumstances of each case before deciding on which side of the dividing line it falls. It is therefore very difficult to generalise about when medical judgment is overruled by a duty to allow a patient access to all the information available.

In the course of his judgment in *Sidaway v Board of Governors of the Bethlem Royal Hospital and the Maudsley Hospital* Lord Bridge, in a passage with which Lord Keith agreed, expressed the view that if there was a substantial risk of an adverse and serious consequence arising (the figure of 10 per cent was suggested), it would be necessary to warn the patient, unless there existed a 'cogent clinical reason' for withholding the information. The risk factor in *Moyes v Lothian Health Board* was 0.2 to 0.3 per cent and *Sidaway* it was within the range of 1 or 2 per cent. In neither case did the court consider that the risk factor was so great as to require that it should be disclosed to the patient.

In assessing the degree of risk of a serious neurological reaction to a patient undergoing angiography, Lord Caplan described the figures of 0.2 to 0.3 per cent as 'a slight risk', and concluded that:

'the risk in such a case falls into the category of cases where the balance of advantage in respect of disclosure or non-disclosure of risk to the patient may well be a matter of fine medical

[44] Ibid.

judgment. It cannot be said that in such a case disclosure of the risk is so obviously required in the patient's interest as to over-ride responsible medical opinion to the opposite effect'.[45]

In *Cosgrove* v *Lothian Health Board*[46] Lord Milligan held that a risk of 0.36 per cent was so slight that a patient would not have refused to undergo an operation even if she had known of the risk.

A doctor, confronted with an emergency, may not have sufficient time to obtain a formal consent. In the case of *Craig* v *Glasgow Victoria and Leverndale Hospitals Board of Management*[47] a surgeon was faced with a dilemma. In the course of an exploratory operation he discovered a carotid body tumour. The task of removing such a growth was complex and carried with it an element of risk. Prior to the operation Mr Craig had given his agreement to the surgeon doing what was necessary. The consent had, however, had been given at the time when it had been believed that Mr Craig had a branchial cyst and the purpose of the surgical intervention had been to confirm this and to take appropriate action. The consultant, with an unconscious patient, required to decide whether to complete the operation or to delay the removal of the tumour until he had an opportunity to explain the nature of the proposed surgical intervention to Mr Craig; having advised him of the risks and dangers involved, he could then seek a fresh consent to proceed. The surgeon decided to continue with the operation and to excise the growth.

Unfortunately one of the possible adverse side effects occurred, and in the subsequent court case Mr Craig argued that his initial consent did not cover the new procedure. The court rejected that contention, holding that the use of the word 'necessary' in the original agreement when describing 'any operation which the surgeon considered necessary' made it a valid consent to what, as a matter of medical judgment, was thought to be an essential and urgent procedure.

The Canadian case of *Lepp* v *Hopp*[48] illustrates that a doctor is obliged to address a patient's concerns in relation to possible difficulties, the experience of the surgeon and the facilities available at the proposed hospital. Although the surgeon knew that the patient had originally wished to have his operation carried out in Calgary instead of in the local hospital, he failed to tell him, first, that the backup facilities in Calgary were far better and, secondly, that this was his first unsupervised operation of this type. When a complication arose, although there was no evidence of negligence *per se*, it was held that the surgeon was liable in damages owing to his failure to advise his patient fully.

[45] Ibid.
[46] 1990 GWD 15-839.
[47] Outer House, unreported, 1st December 1972.
[48] [1980] CLY 2612.

A suggestion that consent forms should be divided into separate sections, with the patient acknowledging his acceptance of each step of any procedure, was rejected in *Davis* v *Barking, Havering and Brentwood Health Authority*.[49] Provided that the terms are clear and the patient has been advised appropriately, a general form will normally be sufficient.

[49] [1993] 4 Med LR 85.

Chapter 5

CHANCES OF FAILURE

As well as advising a patient of any serious risks attached to a procedure or treatment, a doctor or dentist has a legal responsibility to warn that for certain procedures a 100 per cent success rate does not exist. Some operations, however well they may be performed, have a medically recognised number of failures, and provided that a patient has been told of this, and has decided to proceed in the light of that information, no grounds of claim may exist.

Sterilisation
One field of medicine where no guarantee can be given is that of sterilisation. In 1985 a Study Group of the Royal College of Obstetricians and Gynaecologists found that every year 'at least two per thousand sterilisations performed in the UK' fail. Although it is apparent that a proportion of these are due to negligence, a sizeable number of failures occur following perfectly carried out operations. The terms and extent of any warning of possible failure could be important in assessing whether a right of action may exist. Accordingly, the exact wording of any consent form can be a vital piece of evidence. Most forms since 1985 (after *Sidaway* v *Board of Governors of the Bethlem Royal Hospital and the Maudsley Hospital*[1] and the initial hearing in *Thake* v *Maurice*)[2] now include a disclaimer such as: 'I understand that there is a possibility that I may not become or remain sterile.'

It is doubtful whether such a form, even if signed and witnessed, will be enough to discharge a doctor's responsibilities. Given the intended purpose of the operation, a court would require a doctor to explain in some detail the possibilities that the operation may not succeed at all, or that its effect may be only temporary. Advice on continued contraception and clear notes recording what was said to the patient at the time that the consent form was signed would be powerful pointers away from any suggestion that the patient was not properly counselled.

[1] [1985] 1 All ER 643.
[2] [1986] 1 All ER 479.

The requirement to warn about the possibility of recanalisation and therefore pregnancy is an example of how the courts have moved in their approach to the need to disclose information to a patient. In *Waters* v *Park*,[3] decided in 1961, it was held that a doctor who did not warn his patient of the possibility of a sterilisation operation not being totally successful had not been guilty of negligence. When there was a later pregnancy, a claim for damages, which included a claim for the pain and suffering of a second operation, was dismissed. However, in 1996 the action of *Bell* v *Basildon and Thurrock Health Authority*[4] was settled by a payment of £100,000 when, on similar facts to those which had given rise to *Waters*, liability was accepted by the defendants.

The duty to warn of the possibility of a vasectomy failing extends to the patient and his known sexual partners at the time of the operation. A claim following an unwanted pregnancy by the girlfriend of a man who had been advised that his vasectomy had been successful three years before the parties met, failed. The Appeal Court concluded in *Goodwill* v *British Pregnancy Advisory Service*[5] that the duty of care did not extend that far. Thorpe LJ summarised the position:[6]

'The doctor in the circumstances regards himself as advising the patient and, if a married man, the patient's wife. It cannot be said that he knows or ought to know that he also advises any future sexual partners of his patient who chance to receive his advice at second hand. Presented with such a set of facts a doctor is entitled to scorn the suggestion that he owes a duty of care to such a band so uncertain in nature and extent and over such an indefinite future span.'

Cowe v *Lothian Health Board*[7] is an example of a case where, although the notes did not record the terms of any warning as to possible risks nor the taking of a full medical history, the defenders were able to show that, by the deletion of parts of the form, negative answers had been given. The pursuer failed in his claim that the medical problems which had arisen during his vasectomy were due to negligent treatment. He also failed to show that there had been a failure to inquire about an earlier operation. (On the subject of sterilisation, see also chapter 9.)

Disclosure

If something adverse occurs during an operation there may be an obligation on the practitioner to advise the patient. In *Gerber* v *Pines*[8] the defendant left part of a broken hypodermic needle in Mrs Gerber

---

[3] [1961] CLY 5953.
[4] Unreported, 23rd July 1996.
[5] [1996] 2 All ER 161.
[6] Ibid, p 170.
[7] 1993 GWD 18-1171.
[8] (1934) 79 Sol J 13.

when it broke during an injection. He failed to tell her and in a subsequent action it was held by du Parcq J that although there had been no negligence in the initial procedure (the break was caused by a muscular spasm and it was impossible to prevent the needle being absorbed), the doctor was in breach of duty and negligent in not informing the patient immediately. Damages of five guineas were awarded but no costs.

A contrary decision was reached by the Irish Supreme Court in *Daniels* v *Heskin*.[9] The facts resemble those of *Hunter* v *Hanley*[10] in that a needle broke and required to be recovered later by operation. Although the doctor instructed the midwife that if the needle was not found within six weeks an X-ray would be required, he did not inform the patient of the mishap. The court, adopting the approach which was later to form the foundation of Lord Clyde's tests in *Hunter* v *Hanley*, rejected the claim that the doctor had failed in his duties by not advising the patient. They did so on the basis that the doctor had acted in accordance with accepted medical practice.

There are numerous situations where the medical and dental professions are aware, from experience and professional knowledge, that a procedure, however brilliantly and carefully it is carried out, does not guarantee a 100 per cent success rate. In dentistry root canal treatments or fillings do not always prevent later extractions. Similarly, some immunisations do not always totally prevent infection although they may lessen the side effects. Provided the doctor or dentist has not guaranteed success, or where an adverse side effect is a recognised possibility he has warned of this, the mere failure of the procedure will not give a basis for a valid claim.

In *Comber* v *Greater Glasgow Health Board*[11] it was held that a full explanation had been given. It was further held that, because of the parents' trust of doctors, even if there had not been a full explanation of the procedure and risks, the decision to proceed would not have been affected.

Vaccination
During the early 1970s there was a great deal of controversy over the subject of whooping cough immunisation. The government campaigned, by means of advertising and advice, for every baby to be given 'the jag', subject to individual medical advice. Most informed medical opinion agreed that the potential consequences of whooping cough, particularly for a young child, were a far greater risk than any possible side effects of the injection in normal cases. Another smaller body of opinion disagreed and wished the whole campaign stopped.

[9] [1952] IR 73.
[10] 1955 SC 200; 1955 SLT 213.
[11] (OH) 1991 SCLR 904; 1992 SLT 22.

When it appeared that a few babies had become brain-damaged after following the official advice, actions for damages were put in hand. Two cases, one on each side of the border, proceeded. The initial decisions showed a major divergence between the duties imposed by the courts on the Secretary of State for Scotland and on the Health Secretary, who had responsibility for the equivalent programme in England and Wales. In a procedure roll hearing in *Bonthrone* v *Secretary of State for Scotland*[12] Lord Grieve dismissed as irrelevant the claim so far as it was directed against the government minister. In the English action of *Kinnear* v *DHSS*[13] the opposite view prevailed and it was held that a right of action could arise against the Department of Health in relation to the policy of actively encouraging the vaccination programme.

The pursuers in their pleadings in *Bonthrone* v *Fife Health Board*[14] (as it became known after the Secretary of State ceased to be a defender) averred that the Scottish Home and Health Department (for whom the Secretary of State was responsible) had failed to exercise reasonable care in its policy of encouraging routine vaccination for infants against whooping cough without adequately warning parents of the risks involved. They contended that had they been made aware of the possible side effects, they would not have given their consent to their son receiving the injections. As the result of the second inoculation, they contended, the little boy had developed convulsions and was permanently impaired.

Taking their averments *pro veritate*, Lord Grieve concluded that the Secretary of State was discharging his responsibilities

> 'to secure improvement in the physical and mental health of the people of Scotland and the prevention, diagnosis and treatment of illness' (National Health Service (Scotland) Act 1947, s 1).

Section 1 of the National Health Service (Scotland) Act 1972 gave the Secretary of State powers to perform his duties under the 1947 Act. Among those powers were those conferred by s 4(1) to

> 'make such arrangements, to the extent which he considers necessary to meet all reasonable requirements, for the purposes of the prevention of illness'.

And by s 7(1) to

> 'make arrangements with medical practitioners for the vaccination or immunisation of persons against any disease, either by medical practitioners or by persons acting under their direction and control'.

[12] 1987 SLT 34
[13] [1989] CLY 2475.
[14] Outer House, unreported, 30th August 1985.

Because Parliament had given discretion to the Secretary of State to act to the extent he considered necessary in such matters and because, in terms of s 10, 'The Secretary of State [has] power to disseminate, by whatever means, information relating to the promotion and maintenance of health and the prevention of illness', Lord Grieve concluded that unless it could be argued that the Scottish Home and Health Department had not been acting bona fide when it actively encouraged the immunisation programme, no right of action would exist against the government minister.

The 1947 and 1972 Acts were replaced by the National Health Service (Scotland) Act 1978 which, together with the changes brought in by the National Health Service and Community Care Act 1990, represents the current legislative position. Section 1(1) provides that

> 'It shall continue to be the duty of the Secretary of State to promote in Scotland a comprehensive and integrated service designed to secure—
> (a) improvement in the physical and mental health of the people of Scotland, and
> (b) the prevention, diagnosis and treatment of illness'.

The 1978 legislation placed responsibilities on health boards to exercise functions on behalf of the Secretary of State. Section 2(8), as well as giving them (and trusts under the 1990 Act) authority to enforce any rights, also places on them any liabilities, including a claim for damages 'in all respects as if the Health Board were acting as principal' and 'all proceedings . . . shall be brought by or against the Health Board in its own name'.

Section 40 of the 1978 Act replaces previous directions about vaccination and immunisation and gives the minister power to make arrangements with medical practitioners in this field of disease prevention.

In 1990 Lord Milligan was invited to consider whether the Secretary of State could be made liable under the original 1947 Act. The case of *Ross v Secretary of State for Scotland*[15] arose out of a claim by an adult who alleged that as a baby in 1960 he had suffered an adverse reaction to a smallpox vaccination. The judge followed the line taken in *Bonthrone v Fife Health Board*, although the exact issue was different, and concluded that unless it was possible to aver malice, no claim lay against the minister for actions carried out in the discharge of his discretion and in accordance with his statutory duty. Mr Ross's action was therefore unsuccessful.

The action by Mr Bonthrone continued against the remaining three defenders (the GP, the health visitor and her employer, the health

---

[15] 1990 SLT 13.

board). After a lengthy hearing Lord Jauncey assoilzied the defenders, holding *inter alia* that there was no proven connection between the child's tragic condition and the injection. The English action of *Kinnear* v *DHSS* (also known as *Kinnear* v *Wellcome Foundation*) ultimately failed on the same basis. In both cases the courts accepted forceful evidence that there was no proven connection between the whooping cough vaccine and the incidence of convulsions and brain damage in a few young babies.

An action raised in Ireland resulted in a bench reaching an opposite conclusion. In *Best* v *Wellcome Foundation*[16] the court concluded that the pertussis vaccine could cause permanent brain damage, although, as elsewhere, the judges affirmed that it was for the claimant to show that, in his or her particular case, that was what had happened.

The case of *Bonthrone* v *Fife Health Board* illustrates the numerous problems which face a claimant in many medical negligence cases. Mr Bonthrone, suing on behalf of his son, required to show (1) that no doctor would have failed to have warned the parents of the possible side effects, (2) that when his son suffered a reaction to the first injection (and this was disputed), the course of treatment should have been stopped, (3) that if it was the vaccine which had had such catastrophic effects, then even if he could not prove the first point about a warning of side effects being mandatory, any damage resulted from the later injection given after he contended contra-indications were evident, and (4) (and this was essential) that his son's tragic condition was the direct result of the administration of the vaccine.

He lost on every ground and he was left with the *ex gratia* payment of £10,000 which Parliament had authorised, in terms of the Vaccine Damage Payments Act 1979, should be paid to all alleged vaccine victims. The sum now payable to new claimants is £30,000. This is in terms of the Vaccine Damage Payments Act 1979 Statutory Sum Order.[17]

The fact that the Secretary of State had accepted such a claim did not affect the outcome of the civil action. The standard of proof required and the tests to be satisfied were and are totally different. The statutory scheme under the 1979 Act, in terms of s 1(2)(a)-(i), covers vaccinations against a number of diseases. As with similar schemes for pneumo-coniosis sufferers or the innocent victims of contaminated blood, it is intended to provide help without proof of liability, and is administered in a benevolent manner. There is no requirement to prove a direct and positive connection between the injection and the child's illness on a balance of probabilities, nor is it necessary to show that anybody has been at fault.

[16] [1994] 5 Med LR 81.
[17] SI 1991/939.

The contrast with the requirements imposed on a potential pursuer or plaintiff were highlighted in the judgment of Lord Justice Stuart-Smith in *Loveday* v *Renton*,[18] another claim arising from an allegation that the pertussis vaccine had caused brain damage. In his opinion, rejecting the argument that this type of claim fell to be dealt with on the same basis as *McGhee* v *National Coal Board*,[19] the judge, following the views expressed in *Wilsher* v *Essex Area Health Authority*,[20] summarised the true legal position in such a case as follows:

> 'In my judgment the decision makes it clear beyond doubt that the court must decide as a question of fact whether the vaccine can cause permanent brain damage in young children and the onus of doing so rests on the plaintiff and the standard of proof is the balance of probabilities.'

In Scotland attempts to use *McGhee* v *National Coal Board* to lessen the onus on pursuers or to transfer the burden of proof on to the defender in medical negligence cases have met with little success. Lord President Emslie in *Craig* v *Glasgow Victoria and Leverndale Hospitals Board of Management*[21] refused to expand the scope of *McGhee* to include such actions.

Misprescription

Amid the controversy which surrounded whooping cough inoculations, and the final outcome of the Bonthrone's claim, it is easy to lose sight of the fundamental point which applies to all cases arising out of the administration of drugs—as with all medical and dental treatments. If a doctor or dentist is aware of a possible side effect or a potentially adverse reaction, he has a duty to consider what information should be given to the patient. A practitioner who, knowing that his patient drives long distances, fails to warn him of the soporific effects of a particular drug for which he has given a prescription would be negligent. There could be no conceivable reason for not informing the patient, and 'no professional man of ordinary skill would have [failed to do so] if he had been acting with ordinary care'.[22]

In issuing a prescription there is always the possibility of an error, either in the drug selected or in the quantity or frequency of the dosage. In that event a claim may also lie against the pharmacist concerned. Before selecting certain drugs, a doctor or dentist should ensure that the patient is not allergic to it or to any of its derivatives. An obvious example is penicillin, to which some people develop an immediate and dramatic adverse reaction. Any practitioner who fails to inquire as to any such problem before choosing

---

[18] [1990] 1 Med LR 117.
[19] 1973 SC (HL) 37.
[20] [1987] QB 730.
[21] Inner House, unreported, 1974.
[22] 1955 SC 200 at p 206.

a penicillin-based medicine, leaves himself open to a successful claim.

As penicillin is a recognised and generally used drug, it is doubtful whether a pharmacist would be condemned for dispensing a normal prescription. The courts would place the onus on the prescriber (ie, the doctor or dentist) to ensure that the patient had no known allergy. Where, however, the doctor makes an error in the dosage or prescribes something which is dangerous because of, for instance, the age of the person or because of the very cocktail of pills, a pharmacist who ignores that information, or fails to use his own professional expertise, will require to take a share of the liability. What proportion will be attributed to each party depends entirely on the facts.

For many years it was thought that a fair division between prescriber and dispenser was 75/25, on the basis that the doctor or dentist had made the primary error and that the pharmacist had merely complied with a written instruction. The case of *Dwyer* v *Roderick*[23] changed that perception for ever. It is now clear that a court will consider the individual circumstances of each case before apportioning the blame and deciding how to share any liability.

Mrs Dwyer was aged 28 when she developed symptoms which led a GP (Dr Jackson) to diagnose cervical spondylosis, a condition of the neck. Mrs Dwyer's condition did not improve and she was seen at home on two occasions by Dr Roderick, another partner in the GP practice, before an X-ray eliminated the likelihood of the cause of the increasing pain being cervical spondylosis. Dr Roderick then concluded that his patient was susceptible to migraines and prescribed Migril tablets. In 1973 this was a normal method of tackling the complaint. Up to this point no fault attached to either doctor. Dr Jackson's initial diagnosis was reasonable and arrangements had been put in hand to obtain confirmation or otherwise from a radiologist. Dr Roderick's assessment based on the information available to him after the X-ray result was known was medically sound.

In writing the prescription, however, Dr Roderick gave a direction for use which the trial judge described as 'completely and utterly wrong'. It was recognised that Migril was a drug which, if taken in excessive doses, constricted the blood supply to the extremities. Because of this the manufacturers (the Wellcome Foundation) issued every doctor with a leaflet showing the maximum weekly dose as 12 tablets and emphasising that only during an attack should the drug be used. In bold type the text emphasised that the drug should not be taken between attacks. Doctors (including Dr Roderick) were given

---

[23] *The Times*, 12th November 1983.

sufficient copies of the instructions so that any patient starting on Migril could be given one.

Unfortunately Mrs Dwyer was seen in her own home and the leaflets were kept in the doctor's surgery where most prescriptions for Migril were issued. Dr Roderick neither advised her of the risks nor told her when and how often to take the tablets. He never mentioned the existence of the explanatory leaflet.

In what he later described as 'mental aberration', the doctor gave the patient a prescription for 60 Migril tablets to be taken 'Two every four hours, as necessary'. Mrs Dwyer had the prescription made up at her local chemist and started to take the pills four-hourly. Three days later when Dr Jackson visited the patient he found her in a darkened bedroom, as light hurt her eyes. He failed to ascertain what drugs she was taking although certain of the bottles containing pills were on the bedside table. It was not accepted by Dr Jackson that the bottle of Migril tablets with the lethal dosage mentioned on the label was visible.

In the course of six days Mrs Dwyer took 36 tablets. The effect was catastrophic and she suffered permanent damage arising from gangrene. Damages were agreed in 1976 at £100,000 and all that remained was to decide what share fell to be met by whom. Liability was accepted by Dr Roderick's defence society and by the chemist. Both, however, sought to place some of the blame on to Dr Jackson (who, by failing to maintain his defence society membership, was uninsured), and they were unable to agree the division of responsibility between themselves.

At a hearing before Stuart-Smith J the three parties vied with each other to shift as much blame as possible on to the other defendants. The judge, after considering what the effect would have been if Dr Jackson had spotted the error, concluded that Dr Roderick, as the author of the original blunder, should bear 45 per cent of the damages; the chemist, because he dispensed a drug in a dosage which was 'totally inappropriate and wrong', 40 per cent; and Dr Jackson the remaining 15 per cent as by his failure to check the drugs he had prolonged the period during which Mrs Dwyer was overdosing.

Dr Roderick accepted the finding but the other two defendants appealed. Dr Jackson argued that no liability should attach to him and the chemist argued that 40 per cent was an excessive proportion to apply for the dispensing element of fault. Dr Jackson succeeded by a majority in escaping liability (the judges holding that it had not been proved that the Migril bottle was in the room when he was there). As Dr Roderick's advisers had agreed (in an out-of-court offer) to pay 60 per cent of the total and took no part in the appeal hearing, the chemist, who had hoped to leave 15 per cent with Dr Roderick, had to bear 40 per cent (together with most of the costs). The Times Law Report erroneously suggests that the chemist agreed to bear the 15 per cent if Dr Jackson escaped liability; the true position was that the chemist wished his liability reduced to what had, until then, been the norm of 25 per cent. The Appeal Court indicated that had there been any liability attaching to Dr Jackson, the trial judge's assessment of 15 per cent was not one with which they would have interfered. The case is an example of how a claimant's adviser may need to balance various grades of fault when considering tenders which offer to take set percentages of any damages awarded.

Misrepresentation
The handwriting of doctors is notoriously bad. Lawyers trying to decipher almost illegible notes must wonder why there are not numerous claims arising out of errors made by chemists faced with a vague scribble. Pharmacists are trained to clarify any doubts before proceeding so as to ensure that the patient receives what was intended.

Where a chemist failed to decipher a doctor's calligraphy correctly and a patient suffered because of the resulting error, the court in *Prendergast* v *Sam and Dee*[24] held that the doctor's liability should be restricted to 25 per cent, the chemist bearing the rest. The apportionment illustrates the onus which the courts have placed on pharmacists. It also confirms that a doctor or dentist cannot escape liability completely by suggesting that the chemist should have sought clarification before dispensing.

In *Prendergast* v *Sam and Dee* a patient received from his GP a prescription for three items. As the man was an asthmatic they included a ventolin inhaler. The other two items were drugs for the same complaint. One of the drugs was Amoxil but the handwriting was such that the chemist supplied Daonil, a recognised help to diabetics, but a potential danger to others. Mr Prendergast took the Daonil and developed hypoglycaemia. The courts rejected the contention of the doctor that there had been a break in the chain of causation, holding that the initial negligence had been his but concluding that the major proportion of the blame rested with the chemist for failing to check when there was doubt.

The Med LR report contains a copy of the ill-written script, so it is possible to assess, in the same way as the court required to do, whether the chemist should have been in doubt and also whether there was any justification for the interpretation which he came up with.

A Scottish claim which did not proceed as far as a court action was settled in 1981 on a 50/50 basis. A doctor wished to prescribe a particular medicine for a baby. The prescription was meant to show a strength of 37.5 mg. Tragically the decimal point was obscured and the chemist prepared a mixture which was 10 times the appro-

---

[24] [1988] CLY 2425; *The Times*, 14th March 1988; [1989] 1 Med LR 366.

priate dosage for an infant. The baby died and the doctor's insurers had to accept that the poorly written figures had resulted in the pharmacist dispensing a medicine which would have been ideal for an adult but was fatal for a child only a few weeks old. The chemist's advisers agreed that as the prescription revealed the age of the patient, and that the chemist should therefore have queried the dosage, they had to accept an equal share of the agreed solatium for the parents.

High Street chemists, like GPs and dentists, are independent contractors and do not fall under the protection of a health board or a government body. Accordingly a claim against a pharmacist must be against a named individual (or a firm or company if appropriate). As with doctors and dentists, almost every chemist carries professional indemnity insurance. Pharmacists who are employed in a hospital are, of course, in the same position as any other employee of a hospital trust; their employers are vicariously responsible for any acts or omissions.

A nurse also is required to use her professional skill and training in administering drugs. In *Gold* v *Essex County Council*[25] Goddard LJ indicated that a nurse could be regarded as negligent even if she was carrying out the orders of a doctor. The example he chose to illustrate his point was that of a doctor who in a moment of carelessness used a wrong symbol in a prescription and by doing so ordered a dose which an experienced ward sister should have realised was both incorrect and dangerous. If the medicine was administered in such circumstances, some responsibility would rest with the nurse concerned. Lord Goddard added, however, that in an operating theatre it was essential that the surgeon's instructions were followed and that nobody could blame a junior member of the theatre staff for 'unhesitating obedience' in the heat of a crisis.

With health boards now having to accept liability for the mistakes of all their staff, including qualified medical practitioners, the view expressed in *Gold* will be of practical concern only in cases where the NHS is not involved. An error in a private nursing home or clinic could result in a dispute as to how any liability for damages was to be apportioned.

Breakdown in communication
Experience has shown that a large proportion of possible claims and complaints against doctors and dentists arise from a breakdown in communication. It is perfectly natural for a patient to be agitated and upset, particularly if he or she is alarmed by a sudden change in a condition or a fear of a possible diagnosis. This can result in a failure to give the practitioner all the relevant information. Sometimes doctors do not listen to what they are being told—maybe in a garbled

[25] [1942] 2 KB 293.

manner—and omit to probe further to find out the full symptoms and history. It is impossible to lay down how detailed any consultation should be, but it is clear that the courts will not impose on patients an absolute duty to supply every iota of information without prompting or questioning by the doctor.

There is a responsibility on a doctor to obtain appropriate and adequate information before making a diagnosis. There is also a duty to record such information or any findings if another practitioner may need the facts to advise or treat later. Although there is no legal obligation on a doctor to record a patient's history, a failure to do so which results in another doctor being unaware of earlier findings and thus failing to act owing to a lack of information could give rise to a liability. It could fairly be argued that 'no professional man of ordinary skill would have [omitted to make adequate notes for use by a professional colleague] if he had been acting with ordinary care'.

Courts attach considerable importance to contemporaneous notes and this is particularly so in medical negligence cases. As was shown in *Gordon* v *Wilson*[26] it may be that the progress of a tumour can only be seen in retrospect by reviewing the symptoms. Lord Penrose found it is often impossible 'to describe the history of the development of a patient's condition on an objective basis solely on findings from surgery'. He therefore concluded that 'A reliable account of the patient's symptoms from time to time, based on accurate reports and observations, is indispensable in tracing history with any confidence'.[27]

Doctors and dentists use their own shorthand for recording findings and other data. To a colleague these abbreviations and contractions are comprehensible and may reveal a great deal. It is therefore foolish for a lawyer to try to decide, without seeking guidance from a medical or dental expert, whether an apparently brief note in the records contains sufficient information.

Hospital records

It is essential to bear in mind that there are various sources of information in one set of hospital records. As well as the clinical notes, they also include—separately filed—laboratory reports, X-ray findings, a drug cardex, correspondence and the nursing notes. Each is a possible source of information and factors relevant to the care and treatment of the patient may be included in any of them. Only after each has been thoroughly considered can the complete picture be seen.

A large bundle of documents delivered in response to a request or even a specification is not in the same form as it was at the time the patient was being treated (see also p 100 below). Out-patient notes

---

[26] 1992 SLT 849.
[27] Ibid, p 851.

may have been kept in a different department from in-patient notes; nursing notes are kept in the ward and may be separate from the drug cardex showing the doses prescribed; and correspondence with the patient's GP or with other hospitals will have been separately filed. The fact that they are all in one neat folder when the matter calls in court should not mislead anybody into thinking that, at any one time, a doctor has immediate access to all the information.

Sometimes the same information appears in similar form in different parts of the records. This arises because the various elements which make up the file as it appears in court have originally been apart, and some may not have been readily accessible at a particular moment. A patient treated at an accident and emergency department will have the receiving doctor's initial findings and diagnosis recorded on a casualty card. There may be a brief note about whether there was evidence of alcohol consumption and whether the patient could give an account of what happened. If he is discharged, that document will be filed away and even if further treatment is involved there is no guarantee that the casualty card will follow the patient's progress to other departments.

If the patient is to be detained a fresh set of medical notes will be started on his admission to the ward. In the ward there will be a nursing record logging the routine observations and the condition of the patient. This is primarily for the use of the nursing staff and is written by them for their colleagues on other shifts. As a nurse will not immediately have access to the medical notes, some of what is contained in the notes is copied into, or at least summarised on, the nursing Kardex.

One of the reasons for making clear notes in the clinical records it to inform other practitioners of any previous findings so that a change in a patient's condition can be spotted. There is an obligation on a doctor or dentist to communicate with any colleague who may be involved in later treatment.

In *Farquhar* v *Murray*[28] a court allowed a jury trial where there was an allegation that the patient's own 'medical attendant' had failed to give any instructions or message to his replacement while he was away on holiday. The patient had been instructed to poultice his finger until the doctor's next visit, which had been promised for the next day. Instead Dr Murray had gone on holiday and when his colleague finally heard of the patient nine days later (a letter having been sent by a concerned Mrs Farquhar on behalf of her husband), the finger had, because the poultice had been left on for too long, become so infected that amputation was inevitable.

As with all cases alleging medical negligence the success or otherwise of an action based on a failure to communicate will largely

---

[28] (1901) 3F 859.

depend on the individual circumstances. In *Chapman v Rix*[29] a butcher had slipped and stabbed himself with one of his knives. He was seen at a hospital where the doctor considered that he had a superficial wound. He was sent home and advised to contact his own doctor. When the pain increased he did so, telling his GP that the hospital considered his injury to be a minor one. The GP accepted the hospital's conclusions and decided that the patient had a further problem—indigestion.

The butcher died of peritonitis, the knife having penetrated the intestine, but a claim by his widow failed by 4–1 in the House of Lords. It was held that the hospital doctor had not breached a duty of care by not communicating with the GP and that he, in turn, was entitled to assume that a hospital with its facilities would have carried out all the necessary tests before concluding that the wound was merely superficial. The GP had not known that his patient had been at a small cottage hospital with little equipment; hence the instruction to see his own doctor. The decision in *Chapman v Rix* may be particular to its own facts, but as a House of Lords decision, even if from 1960, it still carries weight. Nowadays, however, a Scottish court might be more inclined to follow the strong dissenting judgment given by the only Scot, Lord Keith.

In *Coles v Reading and District Hospital Management Committee*,[30] a case not dissimilar to *Chapman v Rix*, the court found that there was a duty on a hospital doctor to pass on instructions to another practitioner. Mr Coles had attended at a cottage hospital suffering from a crushing injury to his hand. Although advised to go to a major hospital for an anti-tetanus injection he failed to do so. Instead he visited his GP who failed to inquire as to whether he had been immunised and merely changed the dressing. After the patient died of toxaemia it was held that both the hospital doctor (for failing to communicate with anybody) and the GP (for making no inquiries) were at fault.

It is difficult to imagine that in the modern world of instant communication a doctor who failed to pass on a piece of essential information, could escape a finding of fault. It is worth remembering that in *Bonthrone v Fife Health Board* it was accepted that there was a duty on a health visitor to tell a doctor of symptoms which could have been contra-indications to a second whooping cough vaccination.

The law expects all heath professionals to share information which could assist in a patient's treatment. Where the relevant information was contained in X-rays and nursing notes and the medical practitioners failed to examine them for five days, a finding of negligence

---

[29] [1994] 5 Med LR 239.
[30] [1963] CLY 2356; *The Times*, 31st January 1963.

followed in the Canadian case of *Holmes* v *Board of Hospital Trustees of the City of London.*[31]

If the patient's symptoms or complaints are sufficient to put a careful doctor on his guard, and such a doctor would have asked for an X-ray, for example, a doctor who fails to do so could be held to be negligent. In *Johns* v *Greater Glasgow Health Board*[32] a patient attended hospital following a fall. She was diagnosed as suffering from Raynaud's disease aggravated by anaemia. Although the balance of the evidence supported this conclusion, the doctor was held to be at fault because he had overlooked the swelling of both wrists. Both were fractured and by not obtaining an X-ray the practitioner was held to have been negligent.

Medical science and the practitioner's state of knowledge

Medical science advances the state of knowledge of the profession constantly. The results of research and of drug trials and the experiences of practitioners are regularly reported in a host of journals. A doctor or dentist is expected to maintain a knowledge and an awareness of the changes in procedure and of the risks. This was accepted (and reaffirmed by the trial judge, Lord Jauncey) in *Bonthrone* v *Fife Health Board*. A GP needing to advise parents in relation to the benefits and potential problems of pertussis vaccine has to be aware of the up-to-date opinions on such an essential matter. He cannot be expected, however, to study every article in every book or journal.

The test by which the state of knowledge should be measured is that of a careful and competent practitioner in the same field. A specialist will require to have a far deeper knowledge of modern advances and thinking in his particular field than a GP. But just as it would probably be fair to criticise a lawyer who overlooks something covered by an article in the *Journal of the Law Society of Scotland* or in the *Scots Law Times,* a doctor who fails to heed a warning or advice contained in *The British Medical Journal* or *The Lancet* might be considered to be failing in a duty of care.

Lord Denning in *Crawford* v *Board of Governors of Charing Cross Hospital*[33] summarised the position which a court would take and the duty which could be imposed on a practitioner:

> 'It would, I think, be putting too high a burden on a medical man to say that he has to read every article appearing in the current medical press; and it would be quite wrong to suggest that a medical man is negligent because he does not at once put into operation the suggestions which some contributor or other might make in a medical journal. The time may come in a

[31] (1977) 81 DLR (3d) 67.
[32] 1989 GWD 33-1529.
[33] [1953] CLY 2518; *The Times*, 8th December 1953.

particular case when a new recommendation may be so well
known and so well accepted that it should be adopted.'

It is essential to ensure that the state of knowledge being tested is
that at the time of any incident and not that of the date of the proof.
The decisions in *Moyes* v *Lothian Health Board*[34] and *Goorkani* v *Tayside
Health Board*[35] confirm this. It is a viewpoint based on common sense
and the fact that medical knowledge and experience are advancing
daily. New procedures and drugs appear and sometimes a particular
treatment is found to have a previously unrecognised side effect. In
retrospect a particular course of treatment may have been unwise
or even unsafe, but if that is apparent only as the result of hindsight
or a change in expert thinking (perhaps because of further research),
there can be no valid claim. A court will always look to the state of
knowledge and thinking at the time that the treatment was undertaken.

Where the doctor or dentist is a specialist he will be expected to
know and understand the complexities of his own field of expertise.
In *Goorkani* v *Tayside Health Board* Lord Cameron of Lochbroom
was required to consider the position of a doctor who prescribed
Chlorambucil to a patient suffering from Behçet's syndrome. Mr
Goorkani had already lost the sight of one eye and feared total
blindness. The hospital doctor to whom he was referred failed to warn
him that infertility was a possible side effect of the drug. Later tests
showed that Mr Goorkani, the father of one child, had indeed become
infertile. He sued the doctor for omitting to warn him of the possible
consequences of the drug therapy and succeeded in recovering
damages. In assessing the test to be applied the judge stated:[36]

> 'In the present case, it is proper to judge [the doctor] by refer-
> ence to the information and skill which he as a professional
> man possessed at the time when he prescribed the drug
> Chlorambucil.'

A doctor of dentist must act within the range of his competence. If
a problem arises which is outwith it, he must seek help. A failure to
do so, if as a result there is a misfortune which a more experienced
person would have prevented, could be the basis of a successful action.

Although it is possible to lead any doctor or dentist as a witness
with a view to showing what should or should not have been done,
the value of such a witness will vary considerably depending on
certain factors. Scottish courts place the greatest weight (all other
things being equal) on a witness from the same branch of medicine:
see *Scott* v *Highland Health Board*.[37] A judge will expect the person to

[34] 1990 SLT 444.
[35] 1991 SLT 94.
[36] Ibid, p 95.
[37] Outer House, unreported, 29th January 1981.

have comparable experience to the doctor under attack, or at least to be able to speak to the depth of knowledge expected of such a practitioner.

In *Bonthrone* v *Fife Health Board* highly qualified university professors gave erudite evidence about the statistical chances of there being an adverse reaction to a second whooping cough vaccination. Their views no doubt assisted that aspect of the case considerably. Initially, however, Lord Jauncey needed to decide what knowledge of the risks and counter-indications would be expected of a family doctor in a middle-sized practice in an industrial town in 1975 when the child had been vaccinated. For that part of the case the crucial testimony came from two GPs, from practices of similar size to that of the defender, as to what a careful and competent family doctor would have known and done at that time.

The same point emerged in *Hunter* v *Glasgow Corporation*.[38] A young woman was admitted to hospital with problems which had arisen after a home confinement. A junior doctor conducted an exploratory operation and claimed that he had tried to remove a retained piece of placenta. In fact there was no retained placenta and in using 'excessive force' he so damaged the uterus that a hysterectomy was necessary. At the proof before Lord Fraser evidence was led from another junior doctor with comparable qualifications and hospital experience, who was able to describe what he would have done in a similar circumstance. When the judge issued his decision, finding in favour of the pursuer, he placed emphasis on that evidence when assessing whether negligence had been proved.

In *Aird* v *Ramsay*[39] the sheriff looked to the evidence of a general dentist in preference to a hospital consultant for guidance as to the standards and knowledge to be expected from another family dentist.

Proofs or jury trials often take place many years after the events under scrutiny. It is essential that a witness can speak from experience as to the practice and knowledge in that branch of the profession at the relevant time, and that he has kept up to date with developments and progress. If this is not the case, the court may well discount the value of any testimony he gives, and could even refuse to acknowledge him as an expert witness. Such a fate befell a witness in *Moyes* v *Lothian Health Board*.

---

[38] 1971 SC 220.
[39] Glasgow Sheriff Court, unreported, 5th December 1984.

Chapter 6

COMPLAINTS PROCEDURE

It is often difficult at first to determine whether there has been negligence and, even if there has been, whether there is a proven connection between that negligence and any loss. Because the practice of medicine is an inexact science, whether there has been carelessness or just bad luck cannot easily be assessed. Often, unfortunately, the whole circumstances are clothed in mystery and the patient or the relatives are left with a feeling of dissatisfaction.

Doctor/patient relationship

There may be a desire to complain because of a lack of information as to what may have gone wrong. A breakdown in communication is a frequently-heard criticism. Dissatisfaction can also arise from the way in which the situation is handled, particularly if there is a difference of opinion between the doctor and the patient.

Ill manners or even rudeness by a practitioner have never been acceptable. A doctor who resorts to such boorish behaviour is not fulfilling his duty to the patient and an NHS practitioner could be in breach of the terms of service.[1] The decision in *Bennet* v *Scottish Health Board*[2] confirmed that a doctor's responsibilities and duty go beyond attending a patient, correctly diagnosing the complaint and then treating it. With regard to an allegation of aggression and rudeness, the court held that the doctor could be in breach of his duty to the patient.

There is no obligation on a doctor to visit a patient even when a house call is demanded. The decision as to whether to go is a matter of clinical judgment and a GP who decides not to attend cannot be faulted if he can justify his decision on the basis of the information given to him. A doctor's obligation, in accordance with his terms of service, is to give 'all proper and necessary treatment'.[3] It is for him to judge if an immediate home visit is necessary.

---

[1] Every GP is a party to a contract in terms of the National Health Service (General Medical Services) (Scotland) Regulations 1995 (SI 1995/416) which lays down terms of service.

[2] 1921 SC 772.

[3] See note 1 above, para 12.

A doctor's duty to his patient ends with the death of the patient. There is therefore no obligation or legal duty on a practitioner to certify death and issue the appropriate certificate as soon as he is notified. If he is satisfied as a result of information (or from his knowledge of the patient's condition) that death has occurred, the contractual basis created by any terms of service or doctor/patient relationship is terminated. However, the General Medical Council considers that a doctor's duty of confidentiality to his patient continues even after death. Accordingly a practitioner may refuse, even after the patient's demise, to divulge any matters which could be regarded as confidential.

A doctor or dentist cannot, however, refuse to answer relevant questions in court. They cannot plead confidentiality if ordered by a judge to divulge information in their possession. It is possible though for a practitioner faced with such a dilemma to ask the court whether he requires to break a confidence. In *Hunter* v *Mann*[4] Lord Widgery affirmed that a doctor does not have the right to withhold information if called upon to supply it by somebody with the necessary authority. He added, however:[5]

> 'If a doctor is asked a question which he finds embarrassing because it involves him talking about things which he would normally regard as confidential, he can seek the protection of the judge and ask the judge if it is necessary for him to answer. The judge . . . can, if he sees fit, tell the doctor that he need not answer the question. Whether or not the judge would take that line, of course, depends largely on the importance of the potential answer to the issues being tried.'

Lord Widgery's comments were considered in *W* v *Egdell*,[6] a case concerning the confidentiality of the terms of a medical report on a mental patient. The English court confirmed that a doctor does not have the absolute right to silence accorded to lawyers.

Lord Morison's opinion in *AB* v *West of Scotland Blood Transfusion Service*,[7] as the result of which a patient was refused access to records to find the name of a donor in connection with a possible claim, was largely based on the assertion of the requirement for public-interest immunity certified by the relevant minister of the Crown. In the absence of such a certificate the court would require to have weighed the interests of the pursuer against the need to protect the privacy of donors and the danger that other prospective donors might be deterred if they thought that their anonymity could be breached.

[4] [1974] 2 All ER 414; [1974] 1 QB 767.
[5] [1974] 2 All ER 414 at p 420.
[6] [1989] CLY 2357.
[7] 1993 SLT 36.

Formal complaints

Lawyers advising patients often find that the client's initial concern is to lodge a formal complaint, one of the most common charges being that the doctor has refused or failed to explain vital matters. Often, once details have been supplied, the cause of any concern is resolved and there is no need to take matters further.

If an official complaint is being pursued, however, the first question to be considered is against whom the criticism is being made. Prior to April 1996 different bodies were responsible for investigating and dealing with complaints, depending on whether the practitioner was a hospital employee, a GP, a dentist or somebody working outwith the National Health Service. Each body had its own rules and regulations and in some cases there was a very tight time-limit for the lodging of a complaint. On 1st April 1996, as the result of a report by the Wilson Committee,[8] a new system applying to all NHS medical and dental personnel came into effect. It covers any expressed dissatisfaction arising from events after that date. A complaint aired after 1st April 1996 but made in relation to something which occurred between January and March of that year is dealt under the new procedure. Unless written notification was made prior to that date, anything in 1995 or earlier, so far as the complaints procedure is concerned, is time-barred.

Time-limit

The time-limit for lodging a complaint under the post-April 1996 procedure is six months from the incident which gave rise to the dissatisfaction. An exception is made where the patient was unaware of the problem until later. In that event the time-limit is six months from the date of discovering the problem, provided that this is within one year of the incident. (See the National Health Service (General Medical Services) (Scotland) Regulations 1995, as amended.)[9]

This is of particular importance in dental cases where the effect of treatment may not be evident for some time. The period of six months contrasts dramatically with the six-week limit more recently extended to 13 weeks which was rigorously enforced some years ago. (See the National Health Service (General Dental Services) (Scotland) Regulations 1996.)[10]

There is a discretion to extend the time-limit if it appears that, considering all the factors, it was unreasonable for the complaint to be lodged earlier. There is an overriding proviso: it must still be possible to investigate all the facts. In deciding whether to permit an extension, the complaints officer will require to balance how far any delay has prejudiced a full inquiry.

[8] Being Heard, the report of the Review Committee of NHS Complaints Procedure, chaired by Professor Alan Wilson, published May 1994.
[9] SI 1995/416.
[10] SI 1996/177.

If a patient dies after lodging a complaint but before its resolution, a representative can continue with the matter. The same applies if the facts have become the subject of a disciplinary hearing. If the practitioner dies before there is a resolution, the file is closed without any further action so far as the complaints or disciplinary process is concerned. Any claim for damages continues in the normal way against an employer, if appropriate, or the deceased practitioner's executor.

There are transitional arrangements for complaints made before 1st April 1996 but not yet resolved. How such disputes are dealt with depends on how far the procedure had advanced before the new system came into effect. Most will continue to be dealt with under the earlier rules and regulations.

Conciliation

In some situations, as indicated above, the mere airing of a feeling of confusion or dissatisfaction will lead to a satisfactory resolution. A detailed explanation or clarification may be all that is required. For other cases matters will need to be pursued further. The aim of the new process is to allow an early resolution by keeping the two elements of investigation and disciplinary action totally separate.

Every health board have a list of lay conciliators who are willing to assist in effecting a resolution of a difficulty if possible. These people can be approached either by the patient or by the doctor/dentist, but there is no obligation on the other party to accept their ministrations.

Threat of legal action

Under the new procedure, unlike that which prevailed before April 1996, if a patient states that he intends to initiate court proceedings in connection with the matters which are the subject of the complaint, the complaints procedure ceases. This applies only where the threat to take legal action is unambiguous. The official guidance on the implementation of the new NHS complaints procedure, promulgated by the NHS executive, states that the issuing of a lawyer's letter is not automatically a ground for halting the process. Solicitors may, however, wish to avoid any mention of possible litigation if it is hoped to use the complaints procedure to obtain more ammunition for the claim.

Pre-1996 procedure

Before April 1996 a patient wishing to criticise a GP or dentist formally required to rely on the health board, through their chairman, referring the matter to a Service committee. That body, which consisted of 50 per cent practitioners with the balance, including the chairman, being lay members, held a hearing at which legal representation was barred but where the support of a colleague was permitted.

Patients were often at a disadvantage in trying to articulate their position in front of a group half of whom were fellow professionals of the person against whom the complaint was being directed. For the practitioner the fact that the committee had power to recommend a substantial withholding of remuneration meant that few attempts to compromise or apologise were considered for fear that such weakness could influence the possible 'punishment'.

Service committees were only able to deal with cases which arose out of a possible breach of a practitioner's terms of service. Any complaint relating to an issue of clinical judgment was outwith their jurisdiction. This restriction and the fact that there was no compulsion on the board chairman to refer a case to a Service committee if he did not consider that it was justified, resulted in a number of appeals by dissatisfied patients.

This involved an application to the Secretary of State who could set up an appeal body with power to hear the case anew. The same tribunal, which usually consisted of a lawyer and a practitioner, heard appeals if either party was dissatisfied with the findings of a Service committee.

An application to a tribunal at which lawyers were allowed to appear gave both sides a chance to air matters again. However, if a patient was the appellant the task of conducting and financing the appeal fell on his shoulders. Only if a doctor or dentist was the dissatisfied party did the board take over the presentation of the patient's case. Again, there was a possible conflict between the need to resolve a problem and the disciplinary functions of the board.

Complaints officers
Since April 1996 every GP and dental practice has required, in accordance with each practitioner's terms of service, to have a recognised procedure for dealing with complaints. A person must be nominated to administer the process and his name and designation have to be publicised. It is the responsibility of that person (a member of the practice staff) to hear, investigate and endeavour to resolve any dispute. The stated aim is to ensure that 'complaints are dealt with fairly, openly and speedily'. Under the old Service committee system matters could drag on for more than a year.

Health boards and trusts also must appoint a complaints officer with the responsibility of receiving and looking into any complaints made by or on behalf of a patient in relation to the staff or facilities of the board trust. He must be easily accessible to the public and his name and designation, as well as information about where he can be contacted, must be publicised. The complaints officer must follow the course laid down in the written complaints procedure authorised by the board/trust. Arrangements created by that document must be publicised so that patients are aware of their right to criticise and to have all the facts giving rise to any criticism looked into.

Local resolution
Health boards/trusts must have, for each hospital, a local resolution procedure, which should be 'open, fair, flexible and conciliatory'. The primary aim is to try to effect a speedy and satisfactory settlement of a problem; frequently this is achieved orally. The local resolution procedure does not cover cases involving GPs or dentists; for them the practice-based arrangements apply.

Independent review
There is no obligation on a patient to use the above informal methods of seeking satisfaction. If he is dissatisfied with the internal investigation, he can complain to the health board. Again the disciplinary function of that body is kept separate at this point. This part of the process is known as the independent review.

A request for an independent review must be made within 28 days of the completion of the local resolution stage. The request can be made either orally or in writing to any member or employee of the board/trust and does not have to be intimated within the time-limit to the person responsible for considering the application.

Responsibility for examining a complaint made to a health board rests initially with the convener, a non-executive director of the board. His first task is to review the progress of the complaint through any local resolution procedure and to decide what should happen next. He must also decide whether every opportunity to resolve the dispute at the local level has been explored. He has no authority to attempt to resolve any outstanding problems himself. He can, if he considers it appropriate, send the whole matter back to the local complaints procedure level.

If he is of the view that no further progress can be achieved through the initial procedure and that matters remain to be resolved, he can refer the complaint to an independent review panel. This consists of himself, an independent lay member and an independent lay chairman, both nominated by the health board. Each panel is a formally created committee of the health board/trust.

Role of the convener
It is not mandatory for the convener to authorise a hearing by an independent review panel and a patient cannot insist on one being set up. If it is decided that a different course of action is appropriate (including conciliation) or if the convener is of the view that no action or hearing is appropriate, the aggrieved party has no legal power on his own to force a change of approach. He can, however, invite the convener to reconsider his decision. He can also approach the Health

Service Commissioner (ombudsman) who can recommend to the board that a panel should be set up.

The convener is required to put in writing his reasons for declining to direct that a panel should be set up. A copy of his decision and the basis of it must be given to the complainer and to the doctor/dentist. If he does decide to remit a complaint to an independent review panel, he will decide its terms of reference, stating the matters he considers the panel should investigate. Again a copy must be given to both parties.

In laying down the terms of reference the convener will not comment on the grounds of the complaint, nor will he express a view on any earlier discussions which may have taken place at a local level. The panel is able to deal only with matters within the prescribed terms of reference. As those terms are decided by the convener and the patient has no power to vary them, the scope of any investigation may be far more restricted than the patient wishes.

Independent review panel
Special provisions exist for the panel to obtain the advice of independent clinical assessors if, because of the nature of the complaint, this is necessary. Unlike the old Service committees it is possible for the review panel to consider matters of clinical judgment. Its procedure is based on flexibility and informality and its report is sent to the complainer, the practitioner who is the subject of the complaint and the health board.

At any meeting with the panel the complainer (and any other witness, including the practitioner) can be accompanied by somebody of their choosing ('a friend'), unless that person is a legally qualified person acting in that capacity. Previous regulations referred to 'a paid legal representative' but this was circumvented by lawyers claiming that payment by a third party (ie, a support group or a relative) or by a professional body (ie, a defence society) did not count. Accordingly no lawyer, however altruistic his involvement, should take part in such an interview unless he or she is a witness or is a party. The rule covers anybody who is qualified, even if they are not in practice, and can prevent even close relatives participating if they have a qualification in law.

If the chairman agrees, the friend can address the panel on behalf of the complainer or practitioner. The same proviso applies to a wish to talk to the independent assessors if the dispute relates to a matter of clinical judgment; only if the chairman gives his consent can the friend take a speaking role.

The report issued by the independent review panel will set out its conclusions together with any appropriate comments or suggestions. It will not record the deliberations of the members nor will it stray outwith its terms of reference as laid down by the convener. On receipt of the report, the board/trust will consider its terms as soon as possible and must inform the complainer and the practitioner of any action it intends to take as a result of the panel's conclusions.

Disciplinary action

The panel has no authority to suggest to a health board any disciplinary action that it should take. A decision about such action will be taken by the board only when the complaints process is finished and it is for the board alone to decide whether to move into that sphere. If the board decides that disciplinary action is appropriate, the issue is considered by a committee from a different health board, which reports its findings to the original board. A dissatisfied patient has no locus in any such deliberations, nor will the findings be passed to him.

The disciplinary committee does not have access to the findings of the independent review panel and must hear the whole matter from the start. Evidence obtained from a person during the complaints procedure is not admissible and accordingly a patient could find himself relating his story to two different health board bodies—the first concerned with seeking a resolution to the complaint; the second with considering later whether the practitioner was in breach of his terms of service and what, if any, disciplinary action was required.

Health Service Commissioner

Where a person is unhappy about the refusal of a convener to pass a complaint to a panel or an unfavourable finding of a panel, there remains the right to approach the Health Service Commissioner (ombudsman).[11] Since April 1996 he has been able to investigate clinical matters, as well as allegations of maladministration, throughout the NHS.

The ombudsman will not investigate every complaint referred to him and has total discretion whether to act or not. Accordingly if it is intended to involve the ombudsman at any stage, it is vital that every item of relevant information is contained in the initial request to him to investigate.

Among the courses of action open to the ombudsman is to recommend (1) that the whole matter should be referred back to the local resolution process, (2) that a panel should be created to deal with the situation under the independent review procedure, or (3) that in all the circumstances he should take over the investigation and resolution of the problem.

A complaint can be made by an existing or a former patient. It can also be pursued by anybody with the patient's consent. If for any reason the patient is unable to give his consent, then provided the

---

[11] See the Health Service Commissioners Act 1993, as amended.

person has a relationship (whether personal or business) with the patient that would justify the complaint being pursued by that person, no formal consent is required. If the patient could give his consent but chooses to withhold it, the complaint will not proceed further.

Medical records
To enable any independent body or individual to investigate a complaint properly it may be necessary for access to be obtained to a patient's medical records. It is also possible that confidential personal information may have to be revealed. Once a complaint has been made, there is no need to obtain the patient's express consent before such information is released. It can be shown only to those who have a clear need to know in connection with the investigation.

A Code of Practice on the Confidentiality of Personal Health Information[12] issued by the Scottish Home and Health Department sets out the standards of confidentiality in the use and handling of medical records and any personal information disclosed in connection with the investigation and resolution of a complaint. The circular applies at all stages of the procedure. In 1995 the GMC issued its own guidelines[13] on confidentiality. These are in different terms to those contained in the 1990 circular and apply throughout the United Kingdom.

Where there is information in the records emanating from a third party outwith the NHS, then unless that person gives his consent for the information to be passed on, it cannot be seen or considered during the complaints procedure.

Defence societies
Like many disciplinary procedures, those applicable to doctors and dentists do not contain any power to compensate a victim. They may have considerable authority over the practitioner to the extent of damaging or even terminating his career, but if recompense rather than revenge is the ultimate aim, the complaints avenue is of only limited value.

It is also important to realise that in some cases, once the complaint is lodged and accepted, the conduct of proceedings and the pursuit of matters passes out of the patient's hands and is dealt with by the body itself. This is particularly so in the case of the General Medical Council (GMC) and the General Dental Council (GDC). Both bodies, if they choose to investigate a complaint made by or on behalf of a patient or bereaved relatives, take over the matter completely.

They decide whether a particular sub-committee should have the facts referred to it, and their legal team decides what evidence is led

[12] NHS Circular 1990 (Gen/22).
[13] Confidentiality: Duties of a Doctor, issued October 1995.

and what agreements can be made with the advisers of the practitioner. The conduct of the case is entirely outwith the control and influence of the aggrieved party and however angry a patient may be at what he regards as a light disposal, an injured person does not have any say in how things are dealt with. Furthermore, neither the patient nor his relatives have a right of appeal, even if the whole matter is dropped or either body fails or refuses to take any action.

It is reasonable to conclude that although reporting the facts to the GMC or the GDC may satisfy a desire for vengeance, it does not necessarily help to advance the progress of a civil claim for damages. On the contrary, it may cause a delay, because if a defence society is involved on behalf of a doctor or dentist, it will be reluctant to make concessions while it is defending its member's career and livelihood.

A complaint to the GMC or the GDC must be accompanied by a sworn affidavit covering the allegations. Only if there is such a document will either body investigate the matter. Both are based in London and only in quite exceptional circumstances will they hold hearings away from their offices. The GMC is at 178–202 Great Portland Street, W1N 6JE, and the GDC is at 37 Wimpole Street, W1M 8DQ, to where all correspondence should be sent, addressed to the Registrar.

The Medical Act 1983 provides the framework and regulations under which the GMC operates. In 1995 its terms were amended by the passing of the Medical (Professional Performance) Act. It gives the GMC power to require an incompetent doctor to undergo training to ensure his return to standard if there is 'a seriously deficient standard of professional performance'. Similar provisions apply in relation to dentists in terms of the Dentists Act 1984.

The legal system used by both tribunals is that of English law, as was made clear in *McAllister* v *General Medical Council*.[14] In that case the doctor was Scottish, all the alleged events occurred in Scotland and the hearing took place in Glasgow (because of the doctor's medical condition). The GDC also, on one occasion, heard evidence in Scotland in a case which involved a large number of witnesses. A witness appearing before either body may need to be advised about any different rules of evidence or even the form of the oath.

The Scottish Criminal Records Office reports any recordable criminal convictions against a doctor or dentist direct to the GMC or GDC. If a prosecution results in a conviction, no matter what the disposal is, a report will be sent automatically to the appropriate body. The obligation to intimate a criminal court's finding extends to any matter, even one which is totally divorced from professional practice.

An adverse finding by an independent review panel is also frequently reported to the appropriate body. If a complainer fears that no

14 [1993] 1 All ER 982.

action may be taken following the notification, it is always possible to report the facts separately (with the relevant affidavits), but the ultimate decision as to whether to take the matter any further rests entirely with the GMC or the GDC.

Hearings before the GMC or the GDC disciplinary committees usually take place in public and anybody can attend the proceedings. Only the members' deliberations are held in private but their decisions are announced in the presence of the press and the public. In contrast, neither a disciplinary hearing ordered by a health board nor a meeting under any of the various complaints procedures is open to anybody other than the parties concerned.

Both the GMC and the GDC can hear evidence of a sensitive nature in camera and the same applies if a child is a witness. The same rules as would subsist in a court are applicable.

Chapter 7

Fatal Accident Inquiries

In most cases in which medical negligence is alleged, the patient himself is the principal witness. He can speak about the development of the symptoms, what the doctor was told and when, what advice and warnings were given, the extent and scope of any examination and what questions were asked with a view to eliciting more information.

In a case where the patient is dead the task of ascertaining whether the basis of a claim exists is far more difficult. A primary source of information is not available, and inevitably emotions can cloud the thinking of the relatives, who frequently wish to seek somebody to blame. Because of the effects of trauma, advice or information given by a doctor or hospital official at the time may not have been absorbed or understood.

In England and Wales a coroner's inquest usually follows upon any sudden or unnatural death. Although the coroner's power, and particularly the scope available to a jury, has been severely restricted since the days when an adverse verdict was authority for an arrest and criminal charges, an inquest remains a regularly used part of the judicial system south of the border. In particular, unlike the situation in Scotland, it is common to have a coroner's inquest, in public, into cases in which there will obviously be later criminal proceedings.

Seeking an inquiry

In Scotland there is no automatic right to a public inquiry unless the death occurred in the course of the deceased's employment or while he was in legal custody. The widely held belief that there is always a public inquiry if somebody dies within 24 hours of undergoing a general anaesthetic is erroneous. All such deaths are reported by the doctors concerned to the procurator fiscal, but in most cases the file is closed after the facts have been ascertained.

The terms of the Fatal Accidents and Sudden Deaths Inquiry (Scotland) Act 1976, together with the Fatal Accidents and Sudden Deaths Inquiry Procedure (Scotland) Rules 1977,[1] lay down the

[1] SI 1977/191.

circumstances in which fatal accident inquiry (FAI) must be held, as well as the procedure to be followed. Section 6(1) provides the five headings which a sheriff is authorised to cover in his determination, so far as the evidence before him permits.[2]

The first problem faced by anybody advising bereaved relatives is whether to seek an FAI and if so how to achieve it. The original investigations into a sudden or unexplained death are conducted, in private, by the procurator fiscal. After he has gathered all the information and documents with the assistance of the police, he decides whether he requires to report matters to the Crown Office with a view to instigating an FAI. This is because, unless it is compulsory to conduct an FAI—in terms of s 1(1)(a) of the 1976 Act this is restricted to where the death occurred during employment or while in custody—the only person who can invite a court to hold an inquiry is the Lord Advocate. This he is empowered to do, in terms of s 1(1)(b), if the death occurred 'in circumstances in which it appears to [him to] be expedient in the public interest'. He can also decide to seek an inquiry because the death is 'sudden, suspicious or unexplained, or has occurred in circumstances such as to give rise to serious public concern'.

There are therefore two elements which should be satisfied if the Lord Advocate is to seek a public inquiry. The death must be sudden or it requires to be suspicious or unexplained. Furthermore it is necessary for the circumstances to be such that it appears to be in the public interest to have an FAI to enable there to be an investigation.

Many deaths which, had they occurred in England, would have resulted in an inquest, fail to satisfy the criteria of s 1(1)(b). Consequently, in most cases reported to the fiscal, there is no public inquiry—the investigations providing the necessary answers to questions without the need for an FAI—and this is usually in accordance with the wishes of the relatives of the deceased. Where there is still a feeling of dissatisfaction, notwithstanding any explanations which may have been given, there may continue to be a wish for an FAI, but there is no right to demand or insist upon one.

The views of any relatives are taken into consideration before a decision is made in the Crown Office as to whether to seek an FAI. Sometimes an initially adverse decision is reversed as the result of pressure or agitation and an inquiry does take place. The ultimate decision nevertheless lies outwith the hands of the family or their advisers, and factors which do not directly affect the issues which the relatives wish to raise may result in there being no FAI. It is, for instance, extremely rare for there to be an FAI if there are criminal charges outstanding with which the death could in any way be connected.

[2] See 'FAIs—After Lockerbie' 1991 SLT (News) 225.

To guard against possible prejudice in a subsequent criminal trial, a witness giving evidence at an FAI is not obliged to answer any question which could result in an incriminating answer (s 5(2)). Any reply which is given can be founded upon, and all witnesses must answer any relevant questions unless the answer would incriminate the witness himself. If the witness elects not to give an answer the sheriff can order that he does so if he considers that the response could not adversely affect the position of the witness. In *FAI re Marie Coyle*[3] a witness refused to give evidence and would not tell the court his name or age. It was ruled that as a duly cited witness he had to answer all questions unless the reply was covered by s 5(2) and that the ultimate decision as to whether a reply could be compelled rested with the sheriff.

One of the major advantages of an FAI to a family who believe that there may have been medical negligence in connection with their loss is that they can, at public expense, except for the cost of any legal representation, obtain a full hearing of the facts. It is accordingly important not to miss the chance of securing such a hearing, if appropriate, nor should the opportunity to probe deeply be squandered if an FAI does take place.

Legal aid

The Scottish Legal Aid Board (SLAB) has, in the past issued limited certificates to enable relatives to be represented at FAIs. In such cases the application was based on possible reparation proceedings, initially restricted to the cost of attending the inquiry and if necessary ordering a copy of the extended notes of evidence. For the latter a formal application has to be made to the sheriff either at the end of the inquiry or within three months thereafter.

In October 1996 SLAB indicated a change in approach. Certificates are no longer linked to subsequent reparations procedures. Instead, an application can be made purely for representation at an FAI. It will be determined on its merits and will be subject to the same statutory tests as any other application for civil legal aid in terms of Sched 2 to the Legal Aid (Scotland) Act 1986.

This requires an applicant to show that he has a *probabilis causa litigandi* and that it is reasonable in the particular circumstances of the case that legal aid should be granted. SLAB has announced that *probabilis causa litigandi* can be established if the applicant falls within the category of persons entitled to be represented at the FAI, whether as a relative of the deceased, as a potential defender, or even as an accused in later criminal proceedings.

In an important change of policy SLAB has undertaken that the cost of representation at an FAI will no longer be deducted from any damages subsequently recovered in later proceedings.

---

[3] Greenock Sheriff Court, unreported, 12th March 1984.

If there is sufficient evidence to justify an action when the FAI is completed, a fresh application in respect of a reparation action should be lodged. Such a request must be accompanied by the appropriate additional documentation.

Doubts have been expressed as to the appropriateness of granting a legal aid certificate to cover the cost of representation at an FAI unless there is prima facie evidence which will support a claim for or finding of negligence. If the intention is merely to discover why the death occurred, then, unless particularly specific reasons can be produced as to why representation is necessary, it is unlikely that SLAB will grant the sought-for certificate.

Evidence

If the deceased's relatives are represented at the hearing certain factors need to be borne in mind. A sheriff is limited as to what he can include in his findings and it is unlikely that he will permit questions which do not relate to the circumstances of the death. Delays in issuing a death certificate, a failure to notify a close relative, past mistakes or errors in the treatment of other patients have all been ruled as irrelevant matters in an inquiry which has as its sole purpose the investigation of 'the circumstances of *the* death'.

Any party who can show a relevant interest can attend an FAI, be legally represented, ask questions of witnesses, produce documents and reports and if necessary lead evidence. An expert speaking as to what would have been proper practice might be led in such circumstances. He might require, with the permission of the sheriff, to listen to all the evidence before entering the witness box. Often, however, such a specialist is produced by the Crown, which avoids others incurring great expense.

Written statements, if they are signed and affirmed by a witness in the form of an affidavit, may be allowed in evidence. This is permissible only if all those present or represented at the inquiry agree or if the sheriff considers that the allowing of such evidence would not result in unfairness to any of the parties. A copy of the statement should be made available to every party and the terms of any such documents can be referred to by other witnesses, by the parties and by the sheriff in his determination.

If the sheriff allows evidence to be admitted to the FAI by way of affidavit then, unless he directs otherwise, the statement must be read out in court. If this is not done, 'an account shall be given orally of what the sheriff has directed not to be read aloud'.[4]

No corroboration is required to prove a fact in the course of an FAI. This concession to the normal rules of evidence as they existed

[4] Fatal Accidents and Sudden Deaths Inquiry Procedure (Scotland) Rules 1977, rule 10(3).

in 1976 is of little importance now with the relaxation in the standards of evidence which prevail. It does, however, emphasise the terms of the rules, which provide that so far as possible the procedure used at an FAI should be similar to that for a civil case.

Cross-examination

Unlike most other court procedures, there are no rules as to the order in which parties should cross-examine witnesses at an FAI. Most of the evidence is initiated by the fiscal who will ask the opening questions and has a right to re-examine. It may, however, be important to decide who should have the first opportunity to quiz the witness thereafter, and, what is perhaps more important, who should retain the privilege of posing the final queries, with the opportunity to clarify or confuse. The representatives of the health board/trusts and the doctors will probably agree between themselves, depending on who each witness is, the order *inter se*, but it is unlikely that either will voluntarily allow a lawyer representing the relatives the final say.

If agreement as to the order of cross-examination cannot be reached, the sheriff will require to rule. Normal practice is for those representing parties who might be the subject of criticism to be allowed the chance to ask questions last. Similarly, at the end of the evidence it is usual for the representative of the relatives to address the court and to put forward any comments or submissions before those speaking for the doctors, dentists or health workers reply.

Sheriff's determination

At the conclusion of the FAI the sheriff is required, in terms of s 6 of the 1976 Act, to issue a determination. He can choose whether to issue a written decision, as with a sheriff court judgment, to present it orally at the conclusion of the evidence and submissions, or to read it out in court on a date to which the inquiry has been adjourned.

The sheriff requires to follow the five headings contained in s 6(1)(a)-(e). They direct him to set out, as far as is possible:

> '(a) where and when the death or any accident resulting in the death took place;
>
> (b) the cause or causes of such death and any accident resulting in the death;
>
> (c) the reasonable precautions, if any, whereby the death or any accident resulting in the death might have been avoided;
>
> (d) the defects, if any, in any system of working which contributed to the death or any accident resulting in the death; and
>
> (e) any other facts which are relevant to the circumstances of the death.'

There are usually few problems with regard to (a) and (b). The place and time of death are rarely controversial and the terms of the post-mortem report usually give the information needed for (b). Often a sheriff feels unable to do more than issue a formal verdict in view of the limited information given to him, but this need not always be so, provided that appropriate submissions are made seeking findings in terms of the remaining parts of s 6(1).

The terms of s 6(1)(c) are wide and entitle a court to make a finding based on reasonable precautions which, had they been followed, *might* have led to the death being avoided. The use of the word 'might' allows a sheriff to consider almost any possible scenario. Provided the precaution or precautions are reasonable, then as long as there is a remote possibility that their use might have resulted in preventing the death, it is appropriate to seek a finding under this part of the Act.

Section 6(1)(d) is in narrower terms. It is necessary to show not only that there was a defect in the system of working but also that the defect contributed to the death. There is no room for speculation or possibilities; the subsection is expressed in positive terms and nothing short of definite proof that there was a defect and that it caused (or at least contributed to) the death will do. The argument that 'system of work' means that the subsection is applicable only to factory accidents and has no place in a medical FAI has been refuted so often that few agents now even tentatively suggest such a limitation of the sheriff's powers.

Section 6(1)(e) is so wide as to make a vast range of submissions possible. These must relate to the circumstances of the death under consideration; there is no room for general criticism of the NHS, doctors (or dentists), government policy or any other gripe unless it can be shown to be relevant to the question as to how the particular death occurred. It is, none the less, a catch-all subsection of which sheriffs may be happy to be reminded if they are seeking an opportunity to add to an otherwise bare finding.

A determination favourable to a possible medical negligence claim is of considerable assistance in any negotiations prior to court proceedings. Its terms, however, may not be founded upon in any judicial proceedings of whatever nature arising out of the death, nor is it admissible in evidence in any such trial or case (s 6(3)). However, as the Act applies only to Scotland (s 10(6)), it would be possible to use a sheriff's determination in an English court if a way could be discovered to found jurisdiction there.

A copy of the determination can be obtained from the sheriff clerk after it has been delivered. If it is delivered orally at the conclusion of the evidence and submissions, or if the sheriff chooses to read it out in open court on a fixed date, a fee is payable for the copy. If, however, the determination is issued as a normal sheriff court judgment, all interested parties are entitled to a free copy.

Notes of evidence

A copy of the notes of evidence could prove to be invaluable in pursuing a claim later. To obtain legal aid for an action for damages the extended notes are probably essential.

A copy of the notes can be obtained through the court, but only if the application is made within three months of the conclusion of the proceedings. The time-limit is contained in rule 14 of the Fatal Accidents and Sudden Deaths Inquiry Procedure (Scotland) Rules 1977. Any party who took part in the inquiry or who can show a valid interest can obtain a copy of the notes on payment of the appropriate fee to the sheriff clerk.

The modern practice of relying on tape-recording equipment to provide a record of what is said in the course of an FAI places an additional onus on those taking part in the proceedings. In the days when there was a shorthand writer, that person either knew the spelling of complicated medical terminology or insisted that the witness should provide the information required. In the absence of such a system it is essential that agents demand that any word not in common use is spelt out so that the transcribed notes of evidence are both accurate and comprehensible to any expert reviewing them later. Many medical words sound similar but have totally different meanings. The wrong spelling of an important word can lead to confusion if the person reviewing the transcript is unaware of the error.

Judicial review

Although a sheriff's determination cannot be founded upon in any subsequent proceedings arising out of the death, the terms of the findings at the end of an FAI have on two occasions been the subject of a successful judicial review. Until then it had been believed that there was no way of challenging an adverse determination. However, as its terms could not be referred to in evidence at, nor could its provisions be founded upon in, any subsequent judicial proceedings arising out of the death, there was a limit to the damage that such a finding could cause.

The first case to overturn, in part, a sheriff's findings arose out of a death following a road traffic accident. During the course of the argument in the Court of Session in *Lothian Regional Council* v *Lord Advocate*[5] it was never seriously contended that it was not competent to seek to alter a determination made in accordance with the 1976 Act. In his decision Lord Coulsfield pointed out although the Lord Advocate had taken a plea to the competency of the action, that plea had not been insisted upon. He concluded:[6]

[5] (OH) 1993 SCLR 565 (Notes); 1993 SLT 1132.
[6] Ibid, p 1133.

'The Fatal Accidents and Sudden Deaths Inquiry (Scotland) Act 1976 contains no provision for appeal against a determination of a sheriff at such an inquiry. In the circumstances, in my opinion, I am entitled to accept, in the absence of any argument to the contrary, that the present proceedings are competent.'

As a result of the judicial review certain sentences which were highly critical of two road department employees were removed from the determination. The judge rejected an argument that the determination had to stand or fall as a whole and that it was not possible to reduce a part of it. Dealing with this point he stated:[7]

'It appears to me, however, that s 6(1) sets out a number of headings under which particular determinations are to be made and that a determination under one heading need not necessarily be so interlinked with a determination upon another as to make it impossible to separate the two.'

Accordingly there was a precedent when in 1994, in *Smith* v *Lord Advocate*,[8] a petition was presented seeking a judicial review of the findings contained in another sheriff's determination. The case followed an FAI into the death of an elderly lady in Ballochmyle Hospital. It was suggested that she had received inadequate medical care in a nursing home during the months leading up to her admission to hospital. Counsel for two of the doctors who had been severely criticised by the sheriff in his summary were successful at the end of the Court of Session hearing in having certain parts of the determination reduced by Lord Cullen. However, although the judge was unhappy about finding that some of the evidence given by one of the doctors had not been believed ('I am quite unable to understand what justification the sheriff had for forming this view') he did not feel able to change the assessment made by the person who had actually heard the witnesses.

Representation at the inquiry

FAIs can be useful evidence-gathering exercises and if full utilisation is made of the opportunity to clarify the facts and expose problems, it will be far easier to decide whether there is a basis for further action. Representation at the inquiry is therefore essential.

The procurator fiscal is required to serve notice of the inquiry on certain parties, including the nearest relative, but the date, place and time are also intimated in a national and a local newspaper. This allows anybody who can claim to be an interested party to attend, to be represented and to call witnesses. There is no requirement to intimate a list of possible witnesses to any other party, nor in fact is it necessary to give prior notice of an intention to take part in an FAI. In

[7] Ibid, p 1134.
[8] 1995 SLT 379.

terms of the Act, provided a person can satisfy the sheriff that he has an interest in the death, participation is allowed.

Parties who have been found not to have an interest include injured passengers in a vehicle in which the driver was killed (the view being taken that their interest related solely to any claim which they might have rather than to the death itself) and a patient who claimed that he had been the subject of a delay in diagnosis in circumstances similar to those involving the deceased.

An FAI is held in public and the press can and do report the evidence in detail. The only restriction placed on them is a requirement not to reveal details in relation to somebody under the age of 17. The publicity can be very upsetting to close relatives who may be just beginning to get over their loss (an FAI is usually held many months after the death). This is one of a number of factors which need to be considered before a request for an FAI is made.

It is unwise to rely on the fiscal to pursue any allegations of fault himself. Although some do probe with their questions, others take the view that their duty is to lay out the facts in an impartial way, leaving it to a person having a particular line which they wish pursued to do so. Similarly, when all the evidence has been heard some fiscals consider it to be inappropriate for a public official representing the public interest to make submissions outwith the terms of s 6(1)(a), (b) of the 1976 Act. To go further, it has been suggested, would be to exhibit a bias in favour of one party. Only if the evidence showed a matter giving rise to the need for a recommendation in the public interest would such fiscals seek to make a more detailed submission.

It is therefore important that the relatives are represented at the FAI if they wish the death to be investigated fully and if there are questions to which they are seeking answers. The procurator fiscal's office will usually supply copies of the productions or reports, in the same way as it does in a criminal prosecution, so that proper preparation can be undertaken. If appropriate, legal aid can be sought to cover the cost of representation at what can be a lengthy hearing.

One aspect makes an FAI different from a normal court case. As the fiscal is the instigator of the inquiry and accordingly leads most of the evidence, an FAI is the one occasion when an agent does not necessarily have a chance to question his client first. This problem is frequently resolved by the fiscal restricting his questions so as to elicit merely the basic facts, thereby allowing the lawyer to probe with the client the issues which are giving concern.

Further proceedings

When the FAI is over and a decision has been made to pursue an action for damages, that can be done, if necessary, in the same sheriff court. It could even involve a proof before the same sheriff. Such a course was approved in *Black* v *Scott Lithgow Ltd*[9] when an attempt was made to overturn the decision of Sheriff Irvine Smith that he could hear evidence in, and decide upon, a claim by a widow against her spouse's employers after he had presided over and issued a determination following an FAI into the death which gave rise to the claim. In the principal judgment refusing the appeal Lord President Hope pointed out the constraints of s 6(1) when he stated:[10]

> 'There is nothing in this section to make a finding as to fault or to apportion blame between any persons who might have contributed to the accident. . . . It is plain that the function of the sheriff at a fatal accident inquiry is different from that which he is required to perform in a civil action to recover damages. His examination and analysis of the evidence is conducted with a view only to setting out in his determination the circumstances to which the subsection refers, in so far as this can be done to his satisfaction. He has before him no record or other written pleading, there is no claim of damages by anyone and there are no grounds of fault upon which his decision is required. The inquiry is normally held within a relatively short time after the accident. . . . It provides the first opportunity to canvass matters relating to precautions which might have avoided the death or any defects in the system of working which contributed to it, at a stage when these issues have not been clearly focused by the parties to any future litigation which may arise. And it is not uncommon, as happened in the present case, to find questions being asked about possible precautions or defects which are not the subject of averment in the subsequent action of damages.'

After pointing out that the legislation made 'no provision to the effect that the sheriff who conducts a fatal accident inquiry is to be disabled from exercising his judicial functions in relation to any subsequent proceedings arising from the accident' and that as the determination is not admissible in evidence nor can it be founded upon in any judicial proceedings, 'issues which may arise in subsequent proceedings are not to be regarded as having been predetermined by what the sheriff has held to be established at the inquiry',[11] the Lord President opined:[12]

> '[I]t seems to me that there is no sound basis for thinking that a sheriff who has performed his statutory functions under s 6 of the 1976 Act would be unable to apply his mind afresh and with an unbiased mind to the issues raised in civil proceedings which might follow later relating to the same accident.'

[9] 1990 SC 322; 1990 SLT 612.
[10] 1990 SLT 612 at p 615.
[11] Ibid.
[12] Ibid, p 616.

An FAI is no longer a brief court hearing which results in a formal finding. Some inquiries take a number of days or even weeks and result in detailed findings by the sheriff. Those findings, although they cannot be founded upon in any subsequent judicial proceedings, can provide a useful tool in all negotiations. In addition, the evidence on which the findings are based can be referred to in court.

In the same way that an FAI determination cannot be used in later proceedings, neither is it permitted to refer to a finding made in another tribunal. In *FAI re Mary Band*[13] Sheriff Principal Taylor, QC, ruled that a finding by an NHS committee that a doctor had, by failing to attend a patient who subsequently died, breached his terms of service could not be referred to or used in the resulting FAI. The reason was that there was no way of knowing on what basis the committee had reached its view, nor what evidence it had considered. It was impossible to tell whether a full picture had been given to the members of the tribunal, and in any event the tests for a breach of a doctor's terms of service under his NHS contract are totally different from the matters which a sheriff is directed to consider and rule upon in terms of s 6(1) of the 1976 Act.

Because of the very nature of FAIs, and in particular because of the restrictions applying to determinations, FAIs do not appear in the law reports. Sheriff Principal Mowat's decision following the lengthy inquiry into the Lockerbie disaster was, however, analysed and the resulting article[14] may provide a guide as to the limits beyond which a sheriff will not go in an FAI.

At the conclusion of an FAI the procurator fiscal is required, in terms of s 6(4)(b) of the 1976 Act, to send to the Registrar General of Births, Deaths and Marriages for Scotland the name and last known address of the person who has died and the date, place and cause of death. This final detail, in addition to the other facts, is incorporated into a revised version of the death certificate. Although the basic particulars will probably be the same as those that appeared on the original certificate, there may be a fundamental change in the recorded cause of death if the sheriff has enlarged upon his findings in the deter- mination. This could be of importance in any subsequent claim for damages. It may therefore be advantageous to obtain a fresh certificate for lodging in process once the determination terms are known and the Registrar has amended the records.

---

[13] Kirkcaldy Sheriff Court, unreported, 23rd November 1978.
[14] 'FAIs—After Lockerbie' 1991 SLT (News) 225.

Chapter 8

PREPARING A CASE

Prior to 1990 a patient's right to seek a court order for access to his medical records was governed by the terms of the Administration of Justice (Scotland) Act 1972. This, *inter alia*, authorised the recovery of the records prior to the service of a writ in a case where 'proceedings were likely to be brought'. This placed an onus on the potential pursuer and although most doctors and the defence societies supported a policy of voluntary disclosure, it led to some anomalous situations.

Access to records

The passing of the Access to Health Records Act 1990 gave patients and their advisers considerably greater rights to see documents which previously might have been inaccessible. It does not, however, guarantee that all or even some of the documents will be produced. A number of qualifications are contained in the Act and the initial decision on whether to release a file rests with the 'holder of the record'.

The 1990 Act applies to all 'health records', which are defined in s 1 as records which consist of 'information relating to the physical or mental health of an individual who can be identified from that information, or from that and other information in the possession of the holder, and that the record was made by or on behalf of 'a health professional' in connection with the patient's care.

A 'health professional' includes, in terms of s 2 of the 1990 Act, *inter alia* a registered medical practitioner, dentist, nurse, midwife and pharmaceutical chemist. The term also encompasses a scientist employed by a health service body, but only if he is head of a department. No exception is made for health professionals in the public service of the Crown (s 2(4)).

The holder of the records can refuse to grant access to any part or even all of the file if, in his opinion, it would result in the disclosure of 'information likely to cause serious harm to the physical or mental health of the patient or of any other individual' (s 5(1)(a)(i))', or of 'information relating to or provided by an individual, other than the patient, where that person could be identified' (s 5(1)(a)(ii)).

Applying for access

Five categories of person can apply for access to a health record. So far as Scotland is concerned they are listed in s 3(a), (b), (d)-(f). (Section 3(c) refers to the position of children where the record is in England.) The categories are:

'(a) the patient;

(b) a person authorised in writing to make the application on the patient's behalf; . . .

(d) where the record is in Scotland and the patient is a pupil, a parent or guardian of the patient;

(e) where the patient is incapable of managing his own affairs, any person appointed by a court to manage those affairs; and

(f) where the patient has died, the patient's personal representative and any person who may have a claim arising out of the patient's death.'

The Act applies to any document or report written after November 1991. Anything which predates that is, subject to any court order, entirely within the discretion of the record holder, unless it is necessary to refer to a prior document to make sense of later entries. The reason for this apparent anomaly, contained in s 5(1)(b), lies in the fact that until that date entries and comments were placed in the records before there was any expectation that they could be revealed to the patient. Since then every practitioner is presumed to be aware of the terms of the Act and its effects, and to have compiled any documents which fall within its ambit.

(The Access to Health Records Act 1990 should not be confused with the Access to Medical Reports Act 1988. The latter relates to the right of a patient to see any medical report supplied in connection with employment or insurance. It applies only to a document written by a patient's own doctor or by one responsible for his care or treatment. There is, in terms of s 1, a time-limit of six months from the date when the report was issued for any request for access.)

The medical defence organisations favour the voluntary disclosure of the appropriate documents and accordingly for most GPs and dentists a letter requesting a copy of the records, if accompanied by a signed authorisation by the patient, should be sufficient. In regard to health boards and trusts, a letter should be sent to the medical records office. In 1985 all boards were instructed by the Scottish Office that a copy (*note*, not the original) of a patient's hospital records should be provided if the patient or his representative advanced to a hospital official a good reason for needing it.

The practice of offering to deliver a copy of the records to an expert so that he could provide a report for the pursuer's advisers, on condition that the records were not seen by anybody other than the expert, was disapproved by Lord Cameron in *Moore* v *Greater Glasgow Health Board*.[1] He pointed out that to deprive a party or his legal advisers of the chance to consider and examine the records personally is not in accordance with accepted principles.

A doctor or a defence society is entitled to charge a fee for copying the records. If the request is made under the 1990 Act, a maximum fee of £10 is prescribed.[2] It is essential that the basis on which access to the records is sought is clearly stated. Copies of records not covered by the 1990 Act are charged separately.

If the claim arises out of treatment in a private hospital or clinic then, in accordance with guidelines issued in 1992 by the Scottish Office, all medical records of clinical treatment or care while they are maintained by the patient's medical practitioner are held by the hospital, home or clinic. As the doctor is 'an independent contractor', he is the person who will decide whether any part of or even all the notes are covered by the terms of the 1990 Act.

It is important to remember that records may contain a great deal of confidential information as well as irrelevant details. Accordingly a patient's written consent to the release of the information to an outside party, including a lawyer or an independent expert, must be produced before the holder of the records can consider the request.

The consent applies solely to the patient's own records. There is no entitlement to see or consider those relating to anybody else, unless a separate agreement is obtained. This applies to the files of husbands and wives and is an elementary rule which on occasion is broken, giving rise to a potential claim for breach of confidentiality. It may be of considerable interest to a spouse's legal team to have proof of alcohol readings or psychiatric reports relating to an estranged partner, but it is totally wrong if a doctor, in reporting his dealings with a patient, reveals information relating to a husband or wife obtained from that person's file.

Exactly the same situation applies to employers and their employees. Unless there is written consent from a patient, waiving his right to total confidentiality so far as the contents of the records is concerned, the practitioner has no right to reveal or release any part of them unless ordered to do so by a court.

Hospital records
It is sometimes necessary to seek to recover records through the courts using the specification of documents procedure. In the case of hospital records, the application must be intimated to all the parties and served on the Lord Advocate at the Crown Office, 25 Chambers Street, Edinburgh EH1 1LA. Failure to do so will automatically lead to the

[1] 1978 SC 123; 1979 SLT 42.
[2] Section 3(4) and the Data Protection Act 1984, s 21.

dismissal of the motion. This applies whether the case is proceeding in the Court of Session or in the sheriff court.

Although separate documents relating to a patient may be held in various departments of a hospital, one request for their release will suffice. It is for the health board/trust to gather up the X-rays, the medical reports, the pathology department's findings, the nursing notes, as well as the correspondence file, and to package them together.

It cannot be stressed often enough that the manner in which the records are produced for a court is totally different from the manner in which they are held in the hospital. (See also chapter 5, p 66.) Reports and comments which appear side by side in the omnibus file may, during the patient's time in the ward, have been kept separate. Each department and discipline retains its own details in an appropriate place.

This practice can lead to duplication. A common example occurs when a patient with a head injury is taken by ambulance to a casualty department. The paramedics may have been told that the patient lost consciousness briefly, and possibly that will be recorded on the form used by them as '? loss of consciousness'. When the patient reaches the casualty department his details will be noted by a clerk who may copy the statement from the paramedics' summary. Thereafter, when the junior casualty doctor sees the victim, he may not be able—perhaps because the patient is drowsy from the effects of alcohol—to get a full history, so he will rely on the earlier entry and include it on the casualty card. If he consults a more senior colleague for advice as to whether to admit the patient to a ward, that doctor may need to add his view to the medical notes, and to show upon what information he based his decision, he will repeat the earlier note. If the patient is transferred to a ward the casualty department records will not move permanently with him, so the receiving nurse will start her notes with a history which could be a précis of the casualty department findings. The ward doctor must also start a set of notes which will be available for any medical personnel who may be dealing the patient during his stay in hospital. Again the sole source of information may be the casualty doctors' notes.

By now there could be six separate entries in the records referring to a suggestion that the patient had been unconscious. Reading them as a whole one might get the impression that he had told the same story to six people. In fact all the entries had one source: a comment made to a paramedic and copied from one set of notes to another. There is in fact no written proof that the doctors or nurses were ever told anything by the patient. It is thus dangerous to assume that because the same words appear in two or more sections of the notes corroboration of a finding or report exists.

Records kept by a GP or dentist

A patient's records of his treatment by a general practitioner or a dentist are kept by the practice concerned. Application to obtain them should be sent, together with the necessary consent, to the practitioner or to the practice administrator if there is one. If there is a change of GP the records are passed to the new one. The doctor on whose health board list the patient appears (together with the doctor's partners and any designated deputy) is the only GP, except in an emergency or on a temporary basis, who can attend or prescribe for that particular person. A doctor's duty to his patient continues for as long as the name remains on his health board list.

For dentists the position is different. A dentist does not have a health board list of patients. People are free to go to any dentist who is prepared to accept them as patients for a course of treatment. Once that treatment is completed there is no binding or ongoing arrangement; the dentist can decline to embark on another course and the patient can choose to go elsewhere. Accordingly a patient's records are retained by the dentist even if the patient goes elsewhere for treatment.

On a patient's death all GP records are sent to the health board for safekeeping, the name having been deleted from the GP's list. As the records are recalled at the end of the quarter following the death, an application for such a file should be sent to the board if more than three months have elapsed.

Expert opinion

The usual reason for recovering the records is to allow an expert to examine them to see whether there are grounds for commencing proceedings. It used to be common for those advising prospective defenders to offer to send the papers direct to an expert on the condition that nobody else had sight of them. Since the passing of the Access to Health Records Act 1990 any attempt to place a limitation on who can peruse the medical or dental file should be queried. Only if the constraint is required because of a serious risk to the health of the patient or for some other exceptional reason need it be accepted.

It is entirely a matter for a patient and his advisers to choose whom they wish to consult. Unlike the situation in England there is no limit (other than the normal problem of cost) on how many reports are obtained or on the number of experts used.[3] It may be necessary to invite more than one specialist to consider the information before it can be seen whether there is any basis for an action, against whose actings it should be directed and what difference another approach would have made to the outcome.

The Royal College of Surgeons of Edinburgh, the Royal College of Physicians of Edinburgh, the Royal College of General Practitioners

---

[3] But see Lord Caplan's comments in *Moyes* v *Lothian Health Board* 1990 SLT 444 at p 451, final paragraph.

and the Royal College of Physicians and Surgeons of Glasgow each keep a list of experts in specific fields of medicine and dentistry who are willing to provide opinions for prospective claimants. Once an appropriate person has been found he should be approached direct, not through the relevant college.

Because of the constraints imposed by the Civil Legal Aid (Scotland) (Fees) Regulations 1989[4] operated by the Scottish Legal Aid Board (SLAB), it may be necessary to make a number of applications to the Board for increases in expenditure limits or for authority to obtain further information. Medical negligence claims can be complex and the opinion of more than one expert may be essential. Prior approval of the Board must be obtained before an expert can be employed. Bearing in mind that the fees and costs incurred by an expert in perusing all the records and producing a report can be immense, the Board should be informed of the likely expenditure and its approval obtained for the employment of such a person. The regulations do not appear to allow any retrospective sanction.

In view of the size of the outlays the file management should be kept under constant review. Repeated applications for increases in expenditure will probably be inevitable before sufficient facts are confirmed to allow a decision to be made as to whether the basis for a successful claim exists.

In may be necessary to remind SLAB of the terms of *Hunter* v *Hanley*[5] and of the requirement, as seen in *Scott* v *Highland Health Board*,[6] for the expert to be from the correct branch of medicine. A patient's treatment could involve a number of doctors and various specialities. To ascertain whether a claim exists against one or more of them, a specialist opinion by an authority with experience in that field may be necessary. A missed fracture could be due to negligence by the radiologist or the orthopaedic registrar; fault might lie with either, both or neither. Only a radiologist can advise as to whether his colleague should have made the correct diagnosis; only an orthopaedic surgeon can opine on the work of an orthopaedic registrar.

SLAB may be unaware of how essential these opinions are before litigation is embarked upon. A report by a GP may suffice to show the present condition and past treatment, but it is totally inadequate to prove to a court that a surgeon, dentist or gynaecologist has been negligent.

It has been suggested that by doing away with corroboration and allowing hearsay, the Civil Evidence (Scotland) Act 1988 lessened the need for separate expert reports from the various disciplines involved in a medical negligence claim. Such a view is entirely without foundation.

[4] SI 1989/1490.
[5] 1955 SC 200; 1955 SLT 213.
[6] Outer House, unreported, 29th January 1981.

Raising proceedings

Once there is sufficient information by way of statements and reports an application for a certificate to pursue a civil action follows the normal course. It is however vital that the statement accompanying the application, and any expert opinion on which the allegation of negligence is founded, follows the principles contained in *Hunter* v *Hanley* and *Moyes* v *Lothian Health Board*. Without that the health board or the defence society, through their legal advisers, will lodge objections. Past experience has shown that in such circumstances SLAB will refuse the application.

As with any reparation action it is possible (subject to the claim exceeding the summary cause limit) to raise proceedings in the Court of Session or the sheriff court. Although for tactical or other reasons a potential pursuer might wish to choose to fight his case in the Court of Session, the legal aid certificate may state that the proceedings should be taken in an appropriate sheriff court.

The advantages of using the sheriff court lie, at present, in the greater speed of progress of the case and the limitation of expense if legal aid is not available. The principal disadvantage is that it eliminates the possibility of a jury trial, which remains an option under Court of Session procedure. However, although the Rules of Court include such cases as suitable for this mode of proof, the courts have on occasion been reluctant to approve issues. In both *Barr* v *Tayside Health Board*[7] and *Miller* v *Lanarkshire Health Board*[8] the judge held that the complexities of the facts and the special considerations arising from applying the tests in *Hunter* v *Hanley* justified trial by judge alone.

The triennium

If the case is one where it is necessary to invoke the terms of s 19A(1) of the Prescription and Limitation (Scotland) Act 1973 (allowing an otherwise time-barred case to continue), the right to a jury trial is lost (s 19(4)).

As with any claim for reparation, prescription and the running of the triennium have to be considered. Section 17 of the 1973 Act applies as much to medical negligence cases as it does to any claim for personal injuries. A thorough precognition and a detailed examination of the records may reveal when the patient became aware of the three factors mentioned in s 17(2)(b). This could provide a possible escape route should a plea of time-bar be taken if there appears, *ex facie*, to be a gap in excess of that allowed by statute between the date of any act of alleged negligence and the service of the writ.

Sometimes there is a sizeable delay before the true effects of a medical mishap are evident. A patient may wait in vain for signs of

[7] 1992 SLT 989.
[8] 1993 SLT 453.

improvement. It may not be until another doctor or dentist is consulted that there is any indication that matters are not proceeding normally or that there is the prospect of long-term problems ahead. Even then the person may not be aware that grounds for an action exist or may not know where blame lies.

One such situation arose in the circumstances which culminated in *Hunter* v *Glasgow Corporation*.[9] The pursuer's initial case was based on an allegation that a midwife (employed by the first defenders) had failed to ensure that a complete placenta had been expelled during a home confinement. Mrs Hunter had been taken to hospital where a doctor advised her that he had managed to remove the remaining part, but in order to do so had required to damage the uterus, with the result that Mrs Hunter could have no more children. It was only after the three-year time-limit had expired, and after the corporation had adjusted their pleadings and the hospital medical records were recovered, that the possibility that the doctor had blundered became evident. Even in the witness box Mrs Hunter seemed unaware that her claim now included averments against the hospital registrar. Before the hearing of the evidence there was a protracted debate and appeal prior to the court granting Mrs Hunter a proof before answer on her pleadings.

Lord Fraser held at the end of the hearing that the pursuer had had no chance of learning the true position at the time owing to the failure of the doctor to tell her the truth. There had been no retained placenta; a clumsy and inappropriately carried out operation had caused the injury. Mrs Hunter was awarded £2,000 against the doctor.

Had the pursuer's claim against the doctor been dismissed at the earlier hearings, she would have received nothing. The case may be a useful reminder to courts of the particular difficulties which can arise in a medical negligence action and how easily an unfair outcome could follow. It preceded the passing of the Prescription and Limitation (Scotland) Act 1973 so there was no 'equitable' method of circumventing the consequences of time-bar had Lord Fraser not accepted that it did not apply.

Among claims for personal injury, medical negligence cases are perhaps the most likely to make use of the terms s 17(2)(b) of the 1973 Act. The patient, unlike the victim of a road traffic or industrial accident, may not be aware that anything out of the ordinary has occurred. He may have been under a general anaesthetic at the time. Doctors and dentists are under an obligation to inform a patient of any mishap, but some do not. The time-limit runs only from the time when the patient knew or ought to have known (i) that the injuries were sufficiently serious to justify an action, (ii) that they were due to negligence, and (iii) that a particular doctor or

[9] 1971 SC 220.

dentist (or, where appropriate, his employer) can be identified (s 17(2)(b)(i)-(iii)).

If it is impossible to fit the facts within the provisions of s 17, it may be necessary to invite the court to invoke the power contained in s 19A(1) and to override the three-year limit on the ground that it seems, to the court 'equitable to do so'. Although it is impossible to lay down any absolute rules, because each case needs to be considered on its own facts, judges appear to be reluctant to permit s 19A(1) to become an automatic escape route to a dilatory pursuer, no matter how good his case may be.

In *Phillips* v *Grampian Health Board*[10] Lord Clyde was faced with a determined plea of time-bar from the defenders. In 1978 a serviceman had consulted a surgeon in connection with a swollen, tender and hard testicle. A year later he was found to have testicular cancer. He married in 1981 and the following year consulted a lawyer. In 1983 a medical report was obtained and proceedings commenced in 1985, the pursuer having ceased work because of his deteriorating condition. Following his death in 1986 his widow took over the case.

Lord Clyde rejected the pursuer's initial contention that it was not until her husband had received the expert's report, or alternatively when he ceased work, that the claim could be crystallised. He also refused to find that it was 'equitable' that the claim should be allowed to proceed out of time, finding instead that the right to claim had ended in 1982. He concluded that the test used in *Elliot* v *J. & C. Finney*[11] was sound and that where it could be shown that the pursuer could have obtained the necessary information to justify a court writ 'without excessive expenditure of time, effort or money', there were no grounds for exercising the discretion contained in s 19A(1), in favour of the pursuer. *Phillips* v *Grampian Health Board* was decided against the pursuer on all grounds, the judge holding that even if he had exercised his discretion in her favour by overlooking the time-bar, she had failed to show that there had been medical negligence.

An example of a case where there was a likelihood that the pursuer could have been successful if an application to use s 19A(1) had not failed is *Gillespie* v *Grampian Health Board*.[12] Mrs Gillespie cut the middle finger of her right hand and underwent an operation in March 1983. She claimed, and it was not disputed, that during the operation she sustained an injury to her upper arm which caused scarring. Although she received treatment for this from various doctors and hospitals it was not until August 1986 that a claim was intimated. A writ was served on the defenders in November 1986 and after sundry procedure and a lengthy sist to enable her legal aid application to be processed, the pleadings were the subject of a debate in relation to the

[10] (OH) 1991 SCLR 817; [1991] 3 Med LR 16; 1992 SLT 659.
[11] 1989 SLT 208 and 605.
[12] Aberdeen Sheriff Court, unreported, 21st February 1990.

defenders' plea of time-bar. The sheriff held that as Mrs Gillespie had gone into hospital with an injured finger and had left with a scarred arm, there was a *prima facie* case of negligence and that her chances of success were 'very high indeed'. The defenders were 'unlikely to win' and accordingly, as there did not appear to be any particular problem in relation to quantum or with proceeding with a proof despite the delay, he held that it was 'equitable' to permit the pursuer's claim to proceed.

The defenders appealed successfully to the Sheriff Principal. He concluded that the sheriff was wrong to decide that the pursuer's chances of success were so high, and indicated that although it would be for the defenders to put forward an explanation at the proof, it was impossible to predict the outcome until the facts had been ascertained. Because one of the principal reasons on which the original decision had been based had thus been rejected, it was open to the Sheriff Principal to consider the use of s 19A(1) anew.

He summarised the competing arguments.

> '[I]t is in favour of the pursuer that her claim is for a significant sum (£10,000) for an unpleasant injury, which will fail altogether if the action is time-barred since she has no claim against any other person. The other relevant considerations are however in favour of the defenders. If section 19A is applied they will lose the right to have the action dismissed, and whether they win or lose at the proof they will almost certainly have to bear at least their own expenses, since the pursuer is on legal aid and is unlikely to pay any award which may be made against her. The failure to raise the action within the prescriptive period was wholly due to the inactivity of the pursuer. . . . The absence of any explanation means that there is no countervailing equity to set against the prejudice to the defenders of forcing them to defend a time-barred claim.'

He then quoted with approval a passage from Lord Milligan's judgment in *Pritchard v Tayside Health Board*:[13]

> 'The paramount prejudice to the defenders is that to allow the case to proceed would deprive them of the right to have the pursuer's action held time-barred and dismissed. I accept that this is in itself a factor which cannot be outweighed by other than strong equitable considerations in the pursuer's favour.'

As no such considerations existed the Sheriff Principal held that s 19A(1) ought not to be applied to Mrs Gillespie's claim and he granted decree of absolvitor.

Pritchard v *Tayside Health Board* was not a medical negligence case. The pursuer, a nurse, was seeking to make a claim against her employer for an injury arising out of her work. It is significant to

---

[13] 1989 GWD 15-643.

note, however, that Lord Milligan attached importance to her knowledge of medical matters and concluded that the delay in raising the action timeously showed that she had chosen 'not to exercise a right of which she was aware'.

It is evident that the courts will not give more favourable treatment to a pursuer in a medical negligence claim than is afforded to any other litigant seeking the protection of s 19A(1). The results of litigation show how often claims are lost by delay or procrastination.

Chapter 9

CONTRIBUTORY NEGLIGENCE, RES IPSA LOQUITUR AND PUBLIC POLICY

Prior to the passing of the Law Reform (Contributory Negligence) Act 1945, a defender in a reparation action could escape liability by showing that the pursuer had, to any degree, contributed to the outcome by his own negligence. Since then the position has been reversed in that a pursuer can succeed if it is possible to prove that even a small proportion of blame attaches to the defender's acts or omissions, with any damages being reduced by the percentage of fault which attaches to the pursuer.

Contributory negligence

The above principles apply equally to an action based on an allegation of medical negligence. If it can be shown that the pursuer, by his own actions or omissions, contributed in any meaningful way to the outcome, a plea of contributory negligence would be appropriate. A patient who failed to tell a doctor or dentist of a known allergy, even if he had not been specifically asked about it, could find that a court regarded the omission just as negligent as the practitioner's failure to inquire.

A man who knows that he reacts adversely to penicillin cannot avoid a share of the blame if a dentist prescribes an antibiotic which includes the offending derivative and the patient has chosen not to inquire whether the pills contain such a frequently used component. Similarly, the mother-to-be who fails to tell a doctor about a major problem which occurred during an earlier delivery in another hospital (records thus not being immediately available) must accept a share of the responsibility if a difficulty arises which could have been averted had either the doctor sought or the patient volunteered the information.

In *Aird* v *Ramsay*[1] it was argued that a solatium which might be due to the pursuer should be reduced to reflect the fact that she delayed getting treatment after the toothache and pain caused by a fractured reamer commenced. The claim failed on other grounds but in assessing the damages which he would have awarded had Mrs Aird been successful, the sheriff limited them to the period before the delay.

[1] Glasgow Sheriff Court, unreported, 5th December 1984.

Res ipsa loquitur

As has been noted (see p 15), the doctrine of *res ipsa loquitur* does not arise in medical negligence cases as readily as in other reparation actions. In *Mahon* v *Osborne*,[2] which was decided nearly 20 years before the definition of medical negligence was expounded in *Bolam* v *Friern Hospital Management Committee*[3] (and while Lord Hewart's views in *R* v *Bateman*[4] still held sway), the judges were divided as to whether the principle should be invoked.

The action arose from the consequences which followed an operation during which a swab was left in a patient. Scott LJ expressed the view that 'to treat the maxim as applying in every case where a swab was left in the patient seems to me an error of law'. Goddard LJ took a different line, opining that the maxim did apply in such a situation. He summarised his approach thus:

'If, therefore, a swab is left in the patient's body, it seems to me clear that the surgeon is called on for an explanation, that is, he is called on to show not necessarily why he missed it but that he exercised due care to prevent it being left there.'

In 1961 the Privy Council appeared to support Lord Goddard's approach in another case which arose out of a forgotten swab. The opinion delivered in *Cooper* v *Nevill*[5] confirmed that it was negligent to have overlooked the swab and that there had been an unjustified departure from the normal routine.

As has been pointed out elsewhere, because of the form of Scottish pleadings, it is often incumbent upon a defender in a medical negligence case to explain fully what happened and why, despite the most obvious explanation, there is in the circumstances no negligence. Frequently, although the pursuer does not specifically refer to *res ipsa loquitur*, defenders have chosen to offer an explanation as to what has happened. An example of this took place during the hearing of *Steward* v *Greater Glasgow Health Board*.[6]

Mr and Mrs Steward's baby sustained catastrophic brain damage when complications arose during the delivery and they raised an action for damages against the board, alleging that there must have been negligence by their employees, including the obstetricians. The defenders provided a specific explanation and Lord Keith heard detailed evidence from a number of eminent experts from London and elsewhere. The judge accepted their evidence and held that there had been no negligence.

[2] [1939] 2 KB 14. For a modern example of an English court's approach, see *Saunders* v *Leeds Western Health Authority* [1985] CLY 2320.
[3] [1957] 1 WLR 582.
[4] [1925] All ER 45.
[5] [1961] CLY 5951.
[6] Unreported on merits; 1976 SLT (Notes) 66 on quantum.

Recently a plea of *res ipsa loquitur* was pursued in *Gillespie* v *Grampian Health Board*.[7] The court followed the reasoning and approach taken by Denning LJ in *Cassidy* v *Ministry of Health*[8] in which the plaintiff based his claim on the fact that following an operation he had been left with a permanently disabled hand. His position was summarised in the Appeal Court judgment in stark terms: 'I went into the hospital to be cured of two stiff fingers. I have come out with four stiff fingers, and my hand is useless. . . . Explain it, if you can.' The court held that that raised a prima facie case against the hospital authorities. As they offered no explanation as to how it could have happened without there being negligence, the judges held that the defendants had failed to displace the prima facie case against them and accordingly found in favour of the unfortunate Mr Cassidy.

Mrs Gillespie also sought an explanation from a hospital authority after she had acquired an unsightly scar during an operation to repair the flexor tendon of her right hand. Despite treatment she was left with a permanent and embarrassing disfigurement, four inches wide, round almost the entire upper arm. Her position was summarised by the sheriff:

> '[I] went into the defenders' hospital for an operation on [my] hand and came out with an entirely unrelated injury to [my] upper arm, apparently related to the application of a tourniquet. That is not something which should be expected in the normal course of events and it is for the defenders to give an explanation for it.'

It was held at first instance and on appeal to the Sheriff Principal that this was a case where *res ipsa loquitur* applied. Any doubts that such a finding was incompatible with the terms of *Hunter* v *Hanley*[9] were dispelled by Sheriff Principal Ireland: 'I do not regard the decision in *Cassidy* v *Ministry of Health* . . . as inconsistent with the decision of the First Division in *Hunter* v *Hanley*.'

Although Mrs Gillespie lost her case because it was held to be time-barred, the Sheriff Principal dealt with how an action of medical negligence involving *res ipsa loquitur* should be approached by the courts.

> 'In a *res ipsa loquitur* case the pursuer need do no more initially than set out facts raising an inference of negligence. It is then for the defender to aver and prove that he carried out the treatment of the patient with all reasonable care. In support of that he may aver that the treatment was in accordance with accepted and normal practice, and that the injury of which the patient complains is a recognised hazard of the treatment and not

[7] Aberdeen Sheriff Court, unreported, 21st February 1990.
[8] [1951] 1 All ER 574.
[9] 1955 SC 200; 1955 SLT 213.

inconsistent with proper care. If these averments are denied by the pursuer, that raises an issue of fact which can be resolved by proof. It is at that point that the principles laid down in *Hunter* v *Hanley* become relevant. The doctor or surgeon can be held liable only if the method of treatment of the patient was one which no professional man of ordinary skill would have used if he had been acting with ordinary care.'

After dealing with the particular circumstances of the pursuer's action, the Sheriff Principal returned to the subject of the pleadings and what could result from them.

'The effect of the *res ipsa loquitur* doctrine is to shift to the defenders the burden of proving positively that the usual practice was followed. If they do so, and show in addition that the injury to the pursuer was not a foreseeable result of following that practice, it would be difficult (to put it at its lowest) for the court to hold that what the surgeon did was what no professional man of ordinary skill would have done if he had been acting with ordinary care.'

Aird v *Ramsay*, referred to above is an example of a case where a plea of *res ipsa loquitur* was unsuccessful in relation to dental treatment. The court considered that it was for the pursuer to show a departure from normal practice and that the onus of proof had not shifted despite the mishap.

It can therefore be seen that *res ipsa loquitur* will only take a pursuer who can found upon it so far. Its limitations were pithily expressed in *Roe* v *Minister of Health*[10] by Morris LJ:

'[T]his convenient and succinct formula possesses no magic qualities; nor has it any added virtue, other than that of brevity, merely because it is expressed in Latin. . . . It must depend upon all the individual facts and the circumstances of the particular case whether [the doctrine applies].'

Public policy

A court may have an overriding duty to consider questions of public policy when deciding the issues in a case. The English courts have not hesitated on occasions to venture into this area. Scottish judges have been more reluctant although *obiter dicta* views can sometimes be found in the course of a decision.

Failed sterilisation

A subject which causes particular concern is whether it is appropriate to recover damages for the cost of bringing up a child born after a failed sterilisation, assuming that it is possible to prove negligence. On the one hand the parents are incurring considerable costs for which

[10] [1954] 2 QB 66.

they may not have budgeted, on the other it seems to some to be wrong to regard a child as a financial burden in the same way as, for example, extra nursing expenses.

The Scottish courts have recently given two conflicting decisions: *Allan v Greater Glasgow Health Board*[11] and *McFarlane v Tayside Health Board*.[12] In England conflicting decisions in *Udale v Bloomsbury Area Health Authority*[13] and *Thake v Maurice*[14] were, like the above cases, delivered within a short time of each other. One refused to allow a claim for the additional costs of bringing up an unwanted child, the other took the opposite view.

Following rulings by the Appeal Court in *Emeh v Kensington and Chelsea and Westminster Area Health Authority*[15] and *Allen v Bloomsbury Health Authority*,[16] the English courts now appear to be willing to accept certain heads of claim where there has been a 'wrongful birth'. As well as an award to cover the pain, inconvenience and suffering arising from the pregnancy and delivery, a mother can recover a sum to compensate for the additional expense of feeding, clothing and, if appropriate, educating the child, and for the earnings she would have received but for her obligation to bring up the child. The additional strain and pressure of raising a child are normally held to be counter-balanced by the joy of having a healthy baby and observing the progress to maturity. If the infant is handicapped, an additional basis of claim will arise. The courts accept that the task of rearing such a child imposes additional burdens and strains. There is, however, little guidance as to how to calculate the extent of such a claim, nor is it possible to find other than general comments on assessing 'future costs' of upbringing.

Brooke J in *Allen v Bloomsbury Health Authority*[17] expressed the view that a negligent party was liable

> 'to pay for all such expenses as may be reasonably incurred for the education and upkeep of the unplanned child, having regard to all the circumstances of the case and, in particular, to his condition in life and his reasonable requirements at the time when the expenditure is incurred'.

He added that in assessing the period over which the cost of maintenance should be made, 'until the child is 18' would be reasonable.

The case of *Emeh v Kensington and Chelsea and Westminster Area Health Authority* is authority, at least in England, for a right of action

[11] Outer House, unreported, 25th November 1993.
[12] Outer House, unreported, 30th September 1996.
[13] [1983] 2 All ER 522.
[14] [1986] 1 All ER 479.
[15] [1984] 3 All ER 1044.
[16] [1993] 1 All ER 651.
[17] Ibid, p 658.

for any financial loss being available to the father of such a child. It is also clear that the child has no entitlement to sue.

Where there has been a failed sterilisation which is attributable to negligence, the woman can (and the same principle applies in the case of a failed vasectomy), in England, include as part of the claim a figure to compensate for the pain and inconvenience of undergoing a second operation. Although Lord Cameron of Lochbroom disposed of the claim on its merits in *Allan* v *Greater Glasgow Health Board* he held that a claim for the effects of having to undergo a further operation was acceptable. In *McFarlane* v *Tayside Health Board* Lord Gill did not require to address this point as it was not part of the claim. Nothing said in *McFarlane* appears to contradict the view in *Allan* that the pain and inconvenience of a further operation is an acceptable head of claim.

The principles of who can sue and for what applies equally if the unsought-for addition to the family followed a failed abortion or a mis-diagnosis which can be attributed to medical negligence. *Allen* v *Bloomsbury Health Authority* arose from the negligent failure to spot a pregnancy which could have been ended had the true position been discovered in time.

There is no obligation on a woman to seek or obtain an abortion if, owing to a medical blunder, or even to a failure to warn adequately of the possibility of failure, an unwanted pregnancy occurs. Although the judge who issued the original decision in *Emeh* v *Kensington and Chelsea and Westminster Area Health Authority* indicated that a mother who did not pursue the possibility of an abortion had failed to mitigate her loss, this approach was overruled on appeal. Dealing with the defendants' argument that the extent of any damages should be limited, Slade LJ ruled:

> '[No court] should ever declare it unreasonable for a woman to decline to have an abortion in a case where there is no evidence that there were any medical or psychiatric grounds for terminating the particular pregnancy.'[18]

In *McFarlane* v *Tayside Health Board* the defenders abandoned an attempt to argue that there was an obligation on a woman to have an abortion. The opinions expressed by the Appeal Court in *Emeh* v *Kensington and Chelsea and Westminster Area Health Authority* reflect the attitude which the Scottish courts would take on this issue.

As mentioned above, the question as to whether it is open to parents in Scotland to seek damages after the birth of a healthy child where the birth is as the result of medical negligence is the subject of two conflicting decisions. Until the Inner House rules, it will remain difficult to advise a claimant with any certainty.

[18] [1984] 3 All ER 1044 at p 1053.

The judgment in *Allan* v *Greater Glasgow Health Board* approved the English decisions in *Thake* v *Maurice* and *Emeh* v *Kensington and Chelsea and Westminster Area Health Authority* and found that a valid claim could be made under a variety of headings. These included the pain and suffering associated with childbirth, the cost of the layette, a cot, etc, loss of earnings during the pregnancy and for a further 18 months, the cost of converting the house if necessary and the cost of the child's upbringing (which was assessed on the basis of a 7-year multiplier).

Lord Gill rejected that approach in *McFarlane* v *Tayside Health Board*, concluding that 'a normal pregnancy, even if undesired, and the labour with which it ends can [not] be described as a personal injury'. He continued:

> 'In any event, even if pregnancy and labour can be regarded as an injury in a case such as this, I do not consider that that is an injury for which damages are recoverable. The court should not, for the purpose of damages, dissociate pregnancy and labour from their outcome. To do that is to ignore the existence of the child and the happiness that [the mother] has had and will continue to have from her existence.'

He therefore rejected the mother's claim for undergoing 'pregnancy and confinement and the pain and distress of the delivery of [her daughter]'.

He also rejected the claim for any financial losses, past or future, which were a consequence of the birth. Concluding that there is no logical barrier

> 'to the court's concluding in a case such as this that the value of the child's existence will always exceed any costs that may be incurred in bringing him up. . . . In my opinion, the correct principle is that the value of a child should be held to outweigh all such costs'.

In support of that view he quoted the opinion of the court in the American case of *Public Health Trust* v *Brown*[19] and refused to follow *Emeh* v *Kensington and Chelsea and Westminster Area Health Authority* or *Allan* v *Greater Glasgow Health Board*.

He summarised his reasons for doing so by affirming

> 'the principle that the privilege of being a parent is immeasurable in monetary terms; that the benefits of parenthood transcend any patrimonial loss, if it may be so regarded, that parents may incur in consequence of their child's existence'.

The defenders in *McFarlane* v *Tayside Health Board* had invited Lord Gill to give a ruling on whether, as a matter of public policy, a claim for

[19] (388 So 2d 1084 (1980)).

the cost of bringing up a healthy child should be entertained. Although declining to decide the issue on that basis, he indicated that had it been necessary or appropriate to do so, he 'would have had some sympathy with the argument for the defenders'.

An appeal against Lord Gill's reasoning in *McFarlane* v *Tayside Health Board* has been lodged and until the Inner House and, if necessary, the House of Lords, have ruled it is impossible to tell whether *Allan* v *Greater Glasgow Health Board* or *McFarlane* correctly reflects the approach to be adopted by a Scottish court.

Suicide

Questions of public policy also arise in claims involving attempted or successful suicide. Where the basis of an action is a criminal act or something which is offensive to public values, courts have refused to allow anybody to profit. Although it is a number of years since suicide was a crime in England, the Appeal Court refused to allow a crave seeking damages when it was alleged that medical negligence had led to an attempted suicide. *Hyde* v *Tameside Area Health Authority*[20] followed the line taken in New Zealand in *Pallister* v *Waikato Hospital Board*[21] and resulted in the claim being rejected. Lord Denning summarised the court's attitude, commenting:

> 'I feel it is most unfitting that the personal representatives of a suicide should be able to claim damages in respect of his death. At any rate, when he succeeds in killing himself. And I do not see why he should be in any better position when he does not succeed. By this act—in self-inflicting this grievous injury—he has made himself a burden on the whole community. . . . I can see no justification whatever in his being awarded . . . the huge sum of £200,000 because he failed in his attempt. . . . The policy of the law should be to discourage these actions. I would disallow them altogether—at the outset—rather than burden the community with them.'

The other judges, although agreeing that the claim should be repelled, were less absolute in their overall opinions and indicated that it could depend on the particular circumstances of each case.

Mental state of patient

Courts have, however, considered the mental state of the patient in deciding whether to strike out an action. There is a duty on medical and nursing staff to treat the mentally ill, and that treatment could include providing suitable supervision and medication to limit the chances of a mishap. In *Rolland* v *Lothian Health Board*[22] it was accepted that a right of action could exist where a patient, owing to her medical

---

[20] [1981] CLY 1854.
[21] (1974) 1 NZLR 561.
[22] Outer House, unreported, 27th August 1981.

condition, became confused and, because she was not supervised, jumped out of a hospital window, The claim failed, not because of the attempted suicide but because Lord Ross held that the patient's behaviour was not reasonably foreseeable.

In *Barr* v *Tayside Health Board*[23] a nurse who fell and was injured while trying to prevent a disturbed patient from deliberately injuring himself with a broken cup was allowed a proof before answer on his allegation that another nurse had been negligent in not sedating the patient or increasing his supervision. Presumably if the patient had succeeded in his objective a right of action would have existed for him or his relatives because of his known mental state. The risk of a patient attempting to commit suicide and the duties of care involved were considered in *Gill's Curator Bonis* v *Grampian Health Board*.[24]

Interest on damages

Interest on damages often forms a considerable part of any final settlement. Lord Abernethy's ruling in *Purryag* v *Greater Glasgow Health Board*[25] confirmed that interest on past solatium should run at one-half of the relevant court rate—a rate which has, over time, ranged from a high of 15 per cent to the current rate of 8 per cent. It is calculated from the date on which the injury was sustained. This applies even if it results, as it could have done in *Purryag*, in 18 years' worth of interest, nearly doubling the ultimate liability. Lord Abernethy declined to follow the English courts' approach, which is to limit the annual interest rate to 2 per cent.

[23] 1992 SLT 989.
[24] (OH) 1995 SCLR 408 (Quantum).
[25] 1996 GWD 10-584 (on merits); 1996 SLT 794 (on interest).

Chapter 10

CONCLUSION

Advances in medical and dental procedures have meant that far more is now possible in terms of the treatment of patients, with the result that there has been a marked rise in expectations. When these hopes are not fulfilled there is a prospect of litigation.

For many lawyers a medical negligence case can seem like a nightmare, with reports written in an unintelligible language describing procedures which are totally alien. Often the client delays the decision to seek legal advice until late in the triennium, which adds to the pressure.

A claim based on an allegation of medical or dental negligence should not be embarked upon in haste. Much information and many facts have to be gathered before advice can be proffered as to whether there is a chance of success. This may involve getting a number of separate reports, as well as recovering records from a variety of sources.

Seventy-seven per cent of all claims intimated to health boards and defence societies have no chance of success. This statistic has remained constant for a number of years and proves that many lawyers are unaware of the elements needed to obtain an award of damages in such cases. When it is remembered that the 23 per cent which may succeed include cases where liability is not in doubt, it will be appreciated how many hopes are raised only to be dashed later.

The cost of fighting a court action can be immense and even those on legal aid may face a demand for a large contribution. This has to be weighed with the fact that unlike an insurance company which can recover the costs of fighting litigation by increased premiums, the defence societies can and do seek to recoup their expenses directly if an action against one of their members fails. Those who advise prospective litigants have a greater duty than in most other cases to warn of the risks and possible costs of medical negligence litigation.

The courts in Scotland have heard a number of actions during the last 40 years but the principles laid down by Lord President Clyde in 1955 remain the bedrock on which every case will stand or fall. It is

119

impossible to overstate the importance of *Hunter* v *Hanley*[1] in this field of reparation. Virtually every subsequent decision in the Court of Session or the sheriff court contains a reference to the three tests at its heart. It may even be worth supplying a copy of the relevant portion of the judgment to any expert so that there is no doubt as to the strength of the opinion being tendered and the standard against which it will be measured.

If the courts have remained steadfast to the principles of *Hunter* v *Hanley,* judges have had to consider dilemmas which reflect the rapid advances in thinking and knowledge which have taken place, particularly during the last 25 years. Lord Caplan commented in *Moyes* v *Lothian Health Board*[2] that in the course of seven years there had been a complete reversal of attitudes as to how much a patient should be told. The complex issues debated in *Law Hospital NHS Trust* v *Lord Advocate,*[3] the recent 'right-to-die' case, would not have arisen a number of years ago.

Society as a whole is far more questioning and far less willing to accept an adverse consequence following treatment. More and more people, as they read or hear of awards made by British courts, as well as those elsewhere, will want to question their own treatment and that of close relatives, and to inquire whether a possible claim exists.

Medical practitioners are no longer regarded with awe, and this is reflected in the increase in the number of claims and complaints lodged in recent years. Matters which in the past were not pursued are now the subject of requests for legal advice and guidance. Now more than ever, lawyers need to know and understand the various aspects which need to be considered if sound advice is to be given. The days when the average court lawyer rarely needed to consider such matters are now in the past.

Medical and dental litigation is an expanding field, with unchartered territories worthy of exploration. It can be fascinating and rewarding, provided that sight is never lost of the additional complexities which frequently arise. The complexities place such litigation in a different category, which is recognised by the Law Society of Scotland as justifying the certification of specialists in the field. It is, however, a type of court action from which no practitioner needs to flee.

Compared with a normal reparation claim arising from an accident at work there is no difference in the forums available for raising an action based on an allegation of medical negligence. The onus of proof is no higher, nor does the law require a greater number of witnesses. The law is far more settled and secure than in many other fields of

[1] 1955 SC 200; 1955 SLT 213.
[2] 1990 SLT 444.
[3] (IH) 1996 SCLR 491; (OH) 1996 SCLR 566 (Updates); 1996 SLT 848.

litigation and this should make the task of advising on the prospects of success easier.

The assessment of damages is exactly the same as in any other and it is in fact a less intimidating area than at first appears. The use by doctors and dentists of lengthy and unpronounceable words to describe a procedure should not discourage anybody who needs to advise a client. Any medical witness has to be able to explain matters to a judge and possibly to a jury. It is up to a practitioner to ensure that any report is made sufficiently comprehensible so that the obscure is clarified.

The world of medical and dental negligence is undoubtedly different from other areas of legal practice, but it is not unduly difficult or intricate.

Provided the principles of *Hunter* v *Hanley* are always kept in mind and appropriate expert evidence is found to support a claim based on those principles, there is no reason why, even if the number of claims intimated to prospective defenders should fall, the ratio of those which achieve success should not increase.

121

Index